WHY WE MUST
ABOLISH THE INCOME TAX
AND THE IRS

WHY WE MUST ABOLISH THE INCOME TAX AND THE IRS

A Special Report on the National Sales Tax

———

Nelson Hultberg

AFR Publications
Dallas, Texas

The author is grateful for permission to quote material from the following sources:

Excerpt from "GOP: Clinton faced change and 'blinked.'" Copyright © 1995, USA TODAY. Reprinted with permission.

Excerpt from "Ax The Tax" by Stephen Moore. Copyright © 1995 by National Review, 150 East 35th Street, New York, NY 10016. Reprinted by permission.

Excerpts from *Unleashing America's Potential* by the National Commission on Economic Growth & Tax Reform. Copyright © 1995 by The Fund for the Study of Economic Growth and Tax Reform. Reprinted with permission by St. Martin's Press, Inc.

Excerpt from "How Flat Tax Forces Can Win" by Stephen Chapman. Reprinted by permission of Stephen Chapman and Creators Syndicate.

Published by AFR Publications, 10723 Preston Rd., Suite 202, Dallas, Texas 75230

Library of Congress Catalog Card Number: 96-86321

ISBN: 0-9654276-0-9

First Printing, September 1996

The imposition of the [income] tax will corrupt the people. It will bring in its train the spy and the informer. It will necessitate a swarm of officials with inquisitorial powers. It is a direct step toward centralization, of which our Democratic friends profess such horror. It is expensive in its collection and cannot be fairly gathered; and finally, it is contrary to the traditions and principles of republican government.

— Rep. Robert Adams, Pennsylvania
Address to Congress, January 26, 1894

If the Court sanctions the power of discriminating taxation and nullifies the uniformity mandate of the Constitution... it will mark the hour when the sure decadence of our government will commence.

— Justice Stephen J. Field
Pollock v. Farmers Loan and Trust Co., 1894

Unless Americans want to be free, unless they put their tradition of freedom above all else, the Sixteenth Amendment will stay in the Constitution until it wrecks both the tradition and the civilization from which it emerged.

— Frank Chodorov
The Income Tax: Root of All Evil, 1954

Dedicated to the millions of overwhelmed taxpayers throughout America who wish to reclaim the freedom that has been so insidiously and wrongfully wrested from their lives during the past 80 years.

Contents

Introduction

For the greater part of the 20th century, we Americans have been governed from Washington by opportunistic politicians who have made their living extracting ever larger levels of loot from our paychecks in order to build what Frederic Bastiat termed "that great fictitious entity by which everybody tries to live at the expense of everybody else." As a result, our once free nation is now a prodigal, bread and circus regime rapidly approaching the fatal hubris of empire and Caesarism.

Our Founding Fathers heroically attempted to inhibit such hubris with the provisions they wrote into our Constitution that rigidly limited the *levying of income taxes* upon American citizens. The fact that such provisions were circumvented in 1913 is a stellar example of the old saw about the only thing we learn from history is that men don't learn from history.

Any modicum of understanding of the past would have informed the intellectual and political authorities of 1913 that by instituting an *income* tax, they were playing with the same despotic fire that had consumed hundreds of regimes prior to theirs. The Founders knew their history well, while the men of 1913 were myopic and ill-informed. Thus, we got the corporation tax, then the income tax, then the estate tax, then the capital gains tax. As a result, our lives today are fodder for Washington potentates and the special interests.

All this could easily have been avoided if only we as humans would straighten up and learn from history. Every dictatorship that has ever solidified its tentacles around its citizens' lives has used the ability to *tax their income* as its lever to power. Yet despite such glaring historical lessons, we still remain largely impervious to the foibles and disasters of past peoples in their attempts to govern themselves. Such blindness must soon be overcome, or we Americans will surely follow in the wake of all the stultifying tyrannies that tarnish the history of man.

A number of years ago, the eminent sociologist Robert Nisbet wrote about a "new despotism" creeping over us. The great French political economist Bertrand de Jouvenal asked in mid-century, "How is it possible not to see in the stupendous degradation of our civilization, the fruits of state absolutism?" Educator Bernard Iddings Bell warned us that, "The central government has today almost unlimited and anonymous power.... By exercise of the *taxing power*, it dominates all people, all affairs." [1]

The above scholars were not radical extremists out on the fringe of their society. They were sane and sagacious observers of the ominous trends of their time. They could see what fashionable academics and media pundits were refusing to face — that man's eternal tendency to expand government in order to obtain more out of life than he is willing to put in, was once again resurfacing, this time under the guise of *social welfare*. And it was being done through the "taxing power."

What you are going to read in the following pages is an appeal for a new and strictly limited "taxing power" that will check such "state absolutism," and begin the process of giving America back to the people and the original vision of her Founders. The monolith of centralized liberalism in Washington is dead. A vast sea change of opinion has come upon us in the 1990's. But it is still not clearly defined and certain of the path it needs to take. It is hoped that this modest little tract will help Americans better discern that path.

CHAPTER ONE

Tax Philosophy, Fallacies and Facts

Most of us agree there are several vital policies that must be implemented in Washington today in order to check the runaway growth of the Federal Government. A balanced budget, dismantling of numerous bureaucracies, and restoring the Tenth Amendment's authority are three notable examples. But more than anything else, it is with *tax reform* that the future of America lies. Taxes are the hemoglobin of tyranny, without which state power cannot grow. If we wish to truly rein in the omnipresent federal Leviathan, we must concentrate our efforts in the area of taxation — most specifically the *federal income tax.*

As any half-aware high school student knows, the income tax was not a part of the founding of America. The men who gathered in Philadelphia in 1787 to write the Constitution went to great pains to assure their fellow Americans in the 13 states that the Federal Government they were establishing would not have any general power to tax people's income. For the first 125 years of our existence as a country, this view prevailed throughout the land and in Washington. Whatever day-to-day revenues the Federal Government needed would be acquired by other means than taxing the income or property of its citizens. History had taught these early Americans that tyrannical oppression always accompanied a strong central government that possessed an open power to lay direct taxes upon the people's property and income.

Direct taxes are those levied on the specific person who pays them, such as income and property, as compared to *indirect* taxes which are not levied on the person who ultimately pays them, but on products or services and passed on through market activities. Examples of indirect taxes are import, excise and sales taxes. The Founders' intent, as recorded in the Constitutional Convention, was for the Federal Government to rely primarily on indirect taxes for its revenue and only in dire emergencies, such as war, to make use of direct taxes.

The Founding Fathers were firmly committed to keeping the national government strictly limited. Therefore, the government's direct taxing powers were constitutionally checked. Such tax levies had to be drawn from the states and be "apportioned" among them according to each state's population measured by its number of representatives in Congress. As a result, all income taxes had to be written as *specific revenue acts* submitted to the states with their dollar amount and their purpose expressly defined. Each specific act was argued for and against and brought to a vote in Congress. After such a tax was collected through apportionment among the states, its specific power ended. In this way, the Federal Government had no general power to lay taxes perpetually on property or income. It had only limited powers for events such as war that threatened the Republic's existence. [2]

Such a methodology worked well for the first 75 years of our nation's existence. During the War of 1812 and its aftermath, direct taxes on property were levied and apportioned among the states to help pay for the war's costs. After their collection, they then expired.

This strict procedure began to unravel during the Civil War, however. The congressmen of the day and the pundits that supported them were of a subtly different mindset than that of Jefferson and the Founders 75 years earlier. They had begun to drift ideologically toward a more nationalist vision of governing. Justifications for federal intervention to "help develop the expanding nation" increasingly found their way into congressional debates and onto the opinion pages of the newspapers. The stage was set for a radical transformation of power from the states to Washington. The Civil War became a convenient vehicle with which to implement such a transformation.

Since revenue is necessary in order to carry out any expansion of government power, increased taxation was naturally sought. Inevitably, Congress turned its acquisitive attention to the levying of an income tax, justifying its enactment with the necessity of "preserving the Union." The result was the Revenue Act of 1862, which provided for a *graduated* tax of 3 percent on incomes over $600, 5 percent on incomes over $10,000, and 7 percent on any income over $50,000. The *uniformity clause* of the Constitution was expediently ignored by enough members of Congress to assure passage of the tax, which set an ominous precedent. Though the rates were increased with the additional Revenue Acts of 1864 and 1865, the public tolerated the hikes because the overall legislation was written to expire in 1870. At that time, Congress extended its life for two more years and then mercifully let it expire.

The next 25 years were to be a pivotal era in our ideological evolution as a nation. In the 1870's and 1880's, Karl Marx's theories of socialism were beginning to seep into the American culture via the writings of European intellectuals and their stateside sympathizers. These socialist intellectuals dreamed of a *permanent and direct tax on income* that was graduated and redistributive, because it would give them power to enlarge the central government and carry out their vision of collectivizing America's political-economic system. Thus, from the 1870's on to the turn of the century, there were repeated efforts by socialist sympathizers to enact a *permanent* progressive income tax on Americans. Such efforts were upheld by the Supreme Court in 1880 through the magical expedient of simply redefining the income tax into an excise tax, but then rejected as unconstitutional in 1894. All these efforts, however, brought steadily more weakening in the Courts, the Congress, the intellectual community, and the general public toward the ultimate enactment of such a tax.

It is in this historical period between the Civil War's aftermath and the turn of the century that the ground was laid for passage of the famous Sixteenth Amendment in 1913. This amendment finally abolished the constitutional restrictions on income taxation and paved the way for today's *permanent, progressive tax* on our earnings that Washington extracts from our weekly paychecks. In little more than a century, Americans had lost all understanding of the dangerous connection between direct taxation and government aggrandizement.

As a result, for the past 80 years, the Federal Government has had the power to levy direct taxes that never expire on American incomes and to do so without adherence to the *uniformity principle* of the Constitution. This power has grown explosively until it now consumes, when combined with state, city and FICA taxes, as much as 50 percent of the earnings of America's productive people. (A small businessman earning $62,000 is in the 24 percent income tax bracket; he pays 15.3 percent FICA taxes, and often as much as 10 to 12 percent for state and city taxes.)

These taxes are being levied in order to pay for massive personal entitlements, ever-increasing interest on the national debt, automatic welfare handouts, pork barrel projects, farm subsidies, corporation bailouts, foreign aid giveaways, World Bank loans, multi-million dollar congressional pensions, energy industry subsidies, artistic grants, educational controls, mass busing programs, sexual indoctrination programs, wetland protection programs, regional development programs, revenue sharing programs, and hundreds of other needless projects and regimental bureaucracies.

What a far cry all this overweening prodigality is from the Founders' original intent. The vision of Jefferson, Madison and Adams was of a small, strictly contained Federal Government to provide for national defense and certain other expressly stated functions in the Constitution. What has developed instead is an arrogant, bureaucratic *mega-state* spreading its stultifying intrusiveness throughout the land to run roughshod over our rights, our liberties and our productivity.

The purpose of this essay is: 1) to show that such unbridled statism has its primary roots in the power of income taxation; and 2) to lay the foundation for curbing its excesses by demonstrating to Americans the need to replace our federal income tax system with a fair and simple *national sales tax*. If we are to regain control of the Federal Government and genuinely reduce its power over our lives, then we must take away the fuel that allows this monster to expand so voraciously.

The welfare state concept and its ever-mushrooming bureaucracies are rooted in the Marxist scheme of "wealth redistribution" implemented through a *progressive income tax*. Such bureaucracies will never be controlled until the idea of wealth redistribution is fought and overcome. The only way it will be overcome is for enough Americans to join together and demand a repeal of our present federal income tax laws, to be replaced with a national sales tax on goods and services consumed. Such a repeal should be backed by an amendment to the Constitution that abolishes the income tax along with its close cousins, the corporation, capital gains, estate and gift taxes.

Institution of a national sales tax does not *require* a constitutional amendment. A sales tax could be enacted tomorrow merely by congressional vote. The reason for backing such a law with an amendment is to make sure that the income tax and its close cousins are totally eliminated from our lives, and to ensure that future Congresses cannot later reinstate such taxes to gratify momentary majorities.

This could well be a long, drawn out process, however, taking many years to complete. Thus, we should pressure Congress to replace these taxes now with a law mandating a national sales tax and requiring a *two-thirds vote* of both houses to raise any federal tax rates. This would kill the income, corporate, capital gains, estate and gift taxes which will have been reduced to zero. At the same time, we should start proceedings to repeal the Sixteenth Amendment and make general taxation of our income and property unconstitutional again. But we need not wait until the Sixteenth is repealed to enact a national sales tax into law. Such a tax can and should replace the above income taxes immediately.

The rate would be *16 percent* to begin with, but could be readily lowered to *10 percent* if excess federal expenditures are eliminated as the tax base rises through the increased productivity that will accompany abolishment of the IRS and its punitive code of laws and regulations.

The language of the accompanying amendment for the NST should be very clear in stating that all direct taxes (i.e., income, corporation, capital gains, estate, gift and property taxes) will henceforth be prohibited except in time of declared war.

In this way, funding for the Federal Government would be returned to the Founders' original intent, which was that Congress rely on *indirect taxation* such as consumption taxes for its day-to-day operations, and that it be allowed the use of direct taxation on property and income only in time of war or a comparable threat to the existence of the Republic.

This strategy will alarm some conservatives and libertarians who feel we must first abolish the income tax with a constitutional amendment in order to protect ourselves from the danger of Congress later resurrecting the income tax and burdening us with both an income and a sales tax.

These fears are unjustified, for we already live with such a danger. All it would require is a 51 percent vote of our present

Congress to enact a 3 percent sales tax to "help pay for the coming shortfall in Social Security" for example, and in a few years bump it to 5 percent for some other "worthy goal," and then bump it still higher as the years go by. Thus, Congress can saddle us with *both* taxes right now if it wishes. So, by passing the NST into law before we get an amendment, we are not putting ourselves in any danger that we're not already in. Actually we are increasing our protection against being saddled with both taxes because we will then have a *two-thirds vote* requirement in order to legislate a tax increase and resurrect the income tax.

What the Nation is Saying

Radical tax reform is no longer an obscure protest of the political fringe; it has now come to prime time. The runaway growth of the Federal Government and the rogue malevolence of the IRS have finally brought home to a majority of Americans the necessity of taking forthright action. The message we hear from all around the country today is that America has endured an "eighty year national mistake," which desperately needs to be rectified before it buries everyone in a morass of government insanity unseen since the days of Diocletian in 3rd century Rome.

Representative Bill Archer of Texas, Chairman of the House Ways and Means Committee, has stated publicly, "I want to tear the income tax out by its roots. I want to get the income tax out of our individual lives completely.... Fifty IRS agents live in Exxon's headquarters in Houston year-round. There's something wrong with a tax system based on that."[3]

U.S. Senator Richard Lugar of Indiana declared, in launching his campaign for the presidency, "I favor abolishing the federal income tax and all of the Internal Revenue Service apparatus.... I propose to abolish completely the federal individual and corporate tax, capital gains taxes, gift taxes, and inheritance taxes all at the same time. And with them all the loopholes."[4]

"The time has come to revamp the federal tax system," proclaims syndicated columnist Jack Anderson. "I believe it needs a complete overhaul."[5]

Frank Champagne, author of *Cancel April 15th!*, states that, "Our tax system has a price tag exceeding all other forms of government waste by more than 50 percent. We waste over $600 billion a year just to conform to this rat's nest of insane regulations.... Is it any wonder a quiet tax revolution has been going on in America for the past two decades?"[6]

"The tax that was supposed to soak the rich has instead soaked America," writes nationally syndicated columnist Paul Craig Roberts. "The beneficiary of the income tax has not been the poor but big government. The income tax has given us a government bureaucracy that outnumbers the manufacturing work force. It has created welfare dependencies that have entrapped millions of Americans in a dependent underclass that is forced to live a sordid existence of trading votes for government handouts."[7]

David Keating, President of the National Taxpayers Union Foundation, tells us, "More and more elected officials are coming to realize what millions of taxpayers already know: the current federal tax system is a lumbering dinosaur that crushes economic expansion and taxpayer rights under its weight."[8]

"Imagine, just for a moment," exclaims Representative Dan Schaefer (R-Colo.), "that April 15 were just another spring day. What if our tax system required no Internal Revenue Service, had no loopholes for the rich, increased Americans' paltry personal savings rate, encouraged economic investment and weakened special interests' hold on Congress?

"What if it also lowered our trade deficit, made foreign corporations pay U.S. taxes and slowed job flight oversees? ....

"This is not some kind of fantastic Utopia I am describing. It could be reality if America eliminated the personal and corporate income tax system and replaced it with a national sales tax."[9]

The Necessary Revenue

Perhaps the reader is asking himself, "How would we pay for the necessary government functions with just a simple consumption tax? How could we possibly replace income taxes, corporation taxes, capital gains taxes, estate and gift taxes altogether?" Well, surprising though it may be, a 16 percent national sales tax would bring in enough revenue to do just that.

For example, the Federal Government took in $639 billion in 1993 through the combination of income, corporation, capital gains, estate and gift taxes. Replacing these tax revenues would thus require a tax base and rate that would produce $639 billion or more. According to the U.S. Department of Commerce, total personal consumption expenditures (domestic and imported) in America in 1993 were $5,102 billion. Sixteen percent of this figure would be $816 billion, which would be $177 billion more than what is needed.

This surplus would allow Congress the leeway to exempt such mainstay expenditures as food and housing from the base ($1,051 billion) so as to ease the sales tax's burden on lower income earners and still bring in the same revenue received from income, corporate, capital gains, estate and gift taxes. All of these taxes could be abolished and replaced with one 16 percent national sales tax. (Those economic pundits such as Bruce Bartlett and Grover Norquist who dispute these figures are in error. Their mistakes are covered in Chapter Three.)

A revenue neutral national sales tax still leaves us with our present budget deficit, of course. But this problem will never be solved through taxation. What is required is to seriously *cut spending*. Whether the present balanced budget plans in Congress that propose to eliminate the deficit by the year 2002 are "serious" enough remains to be seen.

When Congress submits a budget plan for *one year* that is in balance, we can pretty well figure that it will pan out, barring some major catastrophe. But when Congress submits budget plans for *seven years* into the future that predict balance at the end, it is a far more iffy scenario.

Predicting economic growth and federal revenues over seven years necessitates a *steadily growing* economy for that period without any recessions to foul up the predictions. This is not likely to take place. But at least, Congress has taken a major step toward solving the budget crisis. Whether the spending cuts are "serious" enough, only time will tell.

What Congress needs to grasp, however, is that merely balancing the budget is not going to solve the profound economic problems facing our country today. What is needed is a full scale dismantling of Washington's monster bureaucracies and a restoration of power to the states and freedom to the people. To accomplish this, we must continue sending our politicians dramatic messages as we did in November of 1994. We must tell them we don't just want *more efficient* government; we want *drastically less* government.

Most importantly, we must tell them we want a national sales tax! Imagine what such a simple tax would do for the lives of all Americans. No insufferable record keeping for every purchase, expenditure, salary, gain and loss we incur. No need to chase after legal loopholes, special deductions, and arcane shelters. No endless anxiety over audits. No complex paperwork and computations. No lawyers, no accountants, no bewildering IRS forms to contend with every April. No 17,000 page tax code of legal hieroglyphics to wade through. The snooping, autocratic IRS would be out of our lives forever. Americans would pay their taxes at the cash register as they purchase goods and services throughout the year. The rich would pay more because they consume more. It would be simple, efficient and fair.

Why the Income Tax is Wrong

There are very few people in America, aside from diehard liberals and elite bureaucrats, who will endorse our present income tax system. Most Americans realize that it is grievously flawed. As we have seen, the original intent of the Founding Fathers was to prohibit the use of direct taxes such as an income tax for day-to-day operations of the Federal Government. So the first reason why the income tax should be abolished is that it is contrary to the constitutional principles of *limited government* upon which our nation was founded.

The second and equally important reason why it should be abolished is the stultifying *complexity* of the whole convoluted system. The present IRS Tax Code covers some 17,000 pages of laws and regulations. In addition, the IRS issues endless rulings, notices, procedures, opinions and mandates — all designed to implement hundreds of thousands of pages of court decisions that interpret these 17,000 pages of laws and regulations.

Every year we are inundated with a veritable blizzard of 1040 forms, 2106 forms, 2441 forms, 4136 forms, 4562 forms, 4797 forms, 6251 forms, 8829 forms, 3520 forms, 5471 forms, 8621 forms, TDF 90-22.1 forms — all intertwined with ominous instructions and endless revisions of those instructions, which are in turn intertwined with exasperating schedules A, schedules B, schedules C, schedules D, schedules E, F, SE, and R, etc., etc. Accompanying this blizzard of forms and schedules are a myriad of ever-changing booklets to instruct us on the instructions with hundreds of paragraphs of verbiage and figures that converge into labyrinthine swamps of indecipherable bureaucratese.

Our esteemed members of Congress have, over the past 50 years, constructed an alien and insufferable code of legal jabberwocky so numbing and depressing in its effect that it drives millions of befuddled taxpayers, writhing in anguish every year, into the dens of society's calculators with the green eye-shades where they are promptly skimmed for one more cost in the game of staying alive. How on earth is even a *summa cum laude* from MIT to understand such jabberwocky, let alone all us hoi polloi who struggle with directions for assembling Junior's latest Christmas toy?

Take, for example, the following government obscurantism revealed by David Brinkley in an appropriately titled article, "Baboons In The Moonlight," for the Republican National Committee magazine, *Rising Tide*. The U.S. Treasury instructs us in one of its many directional booklets in this way:

"Subparagraph B in section 1G7, relating to income included on parents' returns, is amended (1) by striking $1,000 in clause I and inserting twice the amount described in 4Aii and (2) by amending subclause (capital II) of clause small ii to read as follows..." [10]

Here we have one more example of how the regimental leg irons of despotism evolve insidiously over the years. They are smuggled into our lives through the disingenuous machinations of tax writing committees in Congress who revel in their power to revise the IRS code every other year so as to reward the gaggles of cronies and special interests that are needed to contribute to said committee member's continual re-election. Such indecipherable jabberwocky is, as Brinkley puts it, "a foreign tongue whose language flows like damp sludge leading from a sanitary landfill." Who can possibly garner any sense from such obfuscation posing as enlightenment?

The IRS experts themselves can no more interpret this morass of complexity in coherent form than a Westerner who doesn't speak Chinese could understand a metaphysical debating society in Beijing. Any two IRS agents are likely to come up with totally opposite viewpoints on any payment or compliance issue far more often than not. The mandatory record keeping and reporting requirements are constantly increasing from one year to the next. Since 1986 alone, there have been over 5,000 changes in the Income Tax Code.

James Dale Davidson, head of the National Taxpayers Union, has estimated that approximately 10 million Americans have dropped out of the system and no longer pay taxes at all. Can anyone blame them? No human being should be subjected to such arbitrary, nonsensical, tyrannical, ever-changing government decrees.

In the National Commission on Economic Growth & Tax Reform report, former IRS Commissioner Shirley Peterson reflects on the state of our federal income tax system. In explaining what must be done, she declares, "It's time to repeal the Internal Revenue Code and start over." [11]

Here in a nutshell is the crux of the problem. The income tax system is beyond broken, and thus it is *beyond fixing*. It does not need to be "reformed." It needs to be "abolished" and replaced with a sounder, saner, fairer means of taxation.

The reason why the system is beyond repair is because it is built upon two fundamentally wrong principles: 1) that *progressive* tax rates and their resulting redistribution of wealth can be used to evoke beneficial changes in society, and 2) that increased government revenue can be achieved by taxing men's profits and productivity.

The first of these erroneous principles (that progressive tax rates are proper tools of social change) conflicts with the original intent of the Founding Fathers. It violates the concept of "equality of rights under the law," which is dramatically enshrined in the Declaration of Independence and is the fundamental axiom of our nation's existence. Because *different classes* of society are assessed *different rates* under a progressive tax system, American citizens are denied an *equal right* to the disposal of their property (i.e., their income) and thus denied equal protection under the laws of the land.

Our country was formed and built upon man's inalienable right to life, liberty and property. How else does one preserve his life, enjoy his liberty and maintain his property than through the production and the consumption of his own income? If the State can take any arbitrary percentage of a man's income it chooses, then that man doesn't have much of a right to the use and disposal of his property, does he? As noted author Richard Maybury has pointed out, he has only the *permission* for that use and disposal, and then only so long as he dutifully serves the State in the manner it deems desirable.

The income tax is evil on many counts, but most heinous is its destruction of the principle of "equality" (i.e., uniformity) because of its progressive nature. If we are to uphold the idea of all men possessing *equal rights under the law*, then there can certainly be no justification for a taxation system that denies men an equal right to the use and disposal of what they earn. Such a system is dictatorial and unconstitutional.

As the renowned Scottish economist, John Ramsey McCulloch, put it in the early 19th century, "The moment you abandon the cardinal principle of extracting from all individuals the *same proportion* of their income or of their property, you are at sea without a rudder or compass, and there is no amount of injustice or folly you may not commit."[12]

Our own Thomas Jefferson astutely summed up such reasoning when he wrote, "The true foundation of republican government is the *equal right* of every citizen, in his person and property, and in their management."[13]

This then is the direction in which all productive Americans must move — toward a *uniform* tax rate. Income taxation itself is dangerous enough to a free society, but *progressive* income taxation is the most nefarious of political policies.

The Socialist Roots

The progressive income tax, from its inception in 1913, was a socialist instrument designed to expropriate the wealth of those who produced it and redistribute that wealth to various factions of society designated as "victims of the capitalist ruling class." Never mind that these "victims of capitalism" were growing better and better off as each decade passed precisely because of the economic growth and opportunity that develops only in a free-market society, while the "beneficiaries of socialism" were growing worse and worse off as each decade passed. Blindness prevailed, and America turned toward the socialist path.

The intellectuals and politicians promoting such redistributions of wealth were driven by warped ideology, but like all government centralizers of history, they also were driven by pursuit of power. From Rexford Tugwell and Huey Long of the thirties to Robert Reich and Hillary Clinton of the nineties, the leftist dream has been a great power drive to transform society into a Utopia of universal equality. "Life will only be fair," they explain, "if the status of the rich and productive is reduced and the status of the poor and inefficient is elevated. Equal rights must give way to equal conditions."

The fallacy in all of this political theorizing is the notion popularized by Karl Marx, that a capitalist society automatically creates an ever-widening disparity of wealth between rich and poor. Thus the claim that society must be equalized in order for its poorer members to become better off. But this is not at all true. Just as a rising tide lifts all boats, so a free-market society lifts *all its citizens* to higher and higher standards of living. This is because it creates ever expanding levels of wealth. Ironically, Marx had it totally backwards. The freer men and women are, the greater the amount of wealth their society will attain. The more bureaucracy, taxation and redistribution (i.e., the more *equalization*) individuals and businesses are saddled with, the poorer their society will become.

If any man doubts that the freer an economy is the wealthier all its citizens will become, he needs only to examine the growth and earnings statistics of America during its "laissez-faire" stage of the 19th century.

We have all been taught in school that this was a dangerous era of exploitation in which the laboring classes were paid bare subsistence wages, and that all workers would have been cursed with a *steadily lowering* standard of living if not for the political reformers at the turn of the century who ushered in a massive, regulatory government with a "progressive" income tax to smooth out the free-market's disparities.

The facts, however, reveal otherwise: As recorded in *The Statistical History of the United States*, real wages for the American working man tripled between the years 1850-1913 (growing from an average of $200 per year to $600), and they did so without heavy federal intervention and without progressive income taxation. There was a 500 percent increase in the Gross Domestic Product from 1870 to 1913. The economy grew at the rate of 4.3 percent annually during this period, which was *four times* the growth rate of previous centuries and is *two times* our anemic growth rate of today.[14]

Workers' real wages were rising at an unprecedented rate in history, where today's real wage growth is totally stagnant. Because there was no income tax, profits for investors and entrepreneurs were exploding. Because there was no Federal Reserve to inflate the money supply, prices were coming down every decade. At the turn of the century, America was the epitome of genuine, *non-inflationary* prosperity. The rising tide principle was working its miracles everywhere, and yet the intellectual, political and financial elites of the country were converting in droves to the Marxist sophistries of "exploitative capitalism." Right at the time when America's system of freedom and individualism was promising to fulfill mankind's economic dreams, it was undercut by Marx's alien and wholly fallacious philosophy of human history.

Marxist theory has consequently led to one of the most pernicious myths of our times: that free-market capitalism, if left alone, will result in the rich and powerful gobbling up the poor and weak. According to leftist intellectuals who have fomented the myth, it is only a large and activist government in Washington that saves us from an economic feudalism of selfish robber barons roaming about subjecting everyone to subsistence-level lives. If highly progressive taxes are not employed to confiscate the wealth of the rich, they allege, we would quickly become a two-class society in which small groups of greedy profiteers enjoy immense fortunes, while large numbers of helpless wage-slaves are left to struggle in penurious misery.

This vision became the common lore of our educational system from 1900 to 1980. It was accepted by almost all teachers, artists, clergymen, journalists, pundits and politicians, and took on the trappings of a sacred dogma not to be challenged.

Thankfully, a small band of brilliant scholars, starting after World War II, began to lucidly and diligently show the fallacies inherent in such thinking. Men like Ludwig von Mises, Friedrich A. Hayek, Milton Friedman, Henry Hazlitt and Murray N. Rothbard produced a vast and dazzling array of works that have thoroughly refuted the socialist paradigm and its variants.

With such scholarly efforts now working their way out into the thinking minds of today's society, we are getting a totally different view of how the world works. We can now see that capitalism is not the exploitative system that the Marxists portrayed it as. In actual fact, capitalism is the great liberator of mankind. We can now see that large, activist governments are not benevolent saviors of mankind, but what they have always been throughout history, suppressors of the vital freedom and ingenuity necessary to create prosperity. We can now see that higher, more progressive tax rates do not create abundance for the poor. They create mastodonic fiefdoms for bureaucrats and destroy the "capital accumulation" necessary to advance society.

The Primary Source of Wealth

Here lies the major key to a nation's prosperity — *capital accumulation*. This is why all free-market countries explode in growth and prosperity for the very workers that liberals claim are victims of marketplace cruelty.

As Ludwig von Mises points out in his classic, *Planning for Freedom*: "American wages are higher than wages in other countries because the capital invested per head of the worker is greater and the plants are thereby in the position to use the most efficient tools and machines.... The economic backwardness of such countries as India consists precisely in the fact that their policies hinder both the *accumulation of capital* and the *investment of foreign capital*. As the capital required is lacking, the Indian enterprises are prevented from employing sufficient quantities of modern equipment, are therefore producing much less per man hour and can only afford to pay wage rates which, compared with American wage rates, appear as shockingly low." [15]

The statist political establishment is fond of claiming that the difference in standards of living between America and its neighbors is due to our superior infrastructure built by government, our array of protective labor laws that provide strong bargaining power for unions, and our progressive legislature that conveys an ever-expanding assortment of benefits and entitlements. In short, left-liberals attribute America's high standard of living to their 20th century agenda of *government activism*.

Such a claim is a profound falsehood. Our high standard of living in America comes from the simple fact pointed out by Mises: working men and women in this country *produce more products and services per man hour* than those in Mexico, Cuba, China or Somalia. The reason they produce more products and services is that they have more sophisticated tools and equipment — computers, backhoes, caterpillars, automated combines, power drills, transport vehicles, etc. — to use in their jobs. A worker with a backhoe can dig and clear far more than a worker with a shovel. An accountant with a computer can service many times more customers than one with a ledger book.

Thus, American workers *earn* more because they *produce* more, and they produce more because our constitutional system has provided protection of private property, which has created vast numbers of entrepreneurs who have been willing to invest their savings to create sophisticated tools and equipment for the employees they hire. As a result, the amount of capital per worker in America is much higher than in Mexico and China. It is this higher "investment per capita" that makes the difference. All this comes about because of individual savers and entrepreneurs who provide the capital to start businesses and then plow their profits back into more and better productive equipment so as to induce growth.

There is also another factor in addition to increased "productivity" that helps to create ever rising wages for all workers in a free-market economy. It has to do with the increased "diversity" that develops as a result of more and more capital accumulation.

As capitalism advanced over the years from the early stages of the Industrial Revolution, it literally exploded in many different areas of productivity, creating multitudinous new job opportunities for laborers of all levels over what they had enjoyed in a simple agrarian economy. Because of this explosive and diversified growth and the marketplace complexity it creates, demand for the laborer's services has dramatically increased over the years. For with the development of such complexity comes the steady establishment of more and more new entrepreneurs and businesses to bid for the available supply of labor. And the only way they can gain laborers for their prospective ventures is to outbid their fellow entrepreneurs by offering higher and higher wages.

It is this ever-increasing *diversity* of new ideas, companies and areas of endeavor, combined with the increasing *productivity* of new tools and technology (all derived from capital accumulation), that gives workers an ever-rising standard of living in a free-market. For such diversity provides workers with a host of different employment opportunities to pit against each other in demand for their services, which makes them more powerful players in the market and allows them to extract ever-higher wages. It also exposes the Marxist claim — that capitalism must bid down wages to bare subsistence levels — as a fallacy on a par with Malthus' population theory.

A basic economic truism can be established here, which can be stated as follows: As long as the "diversity" and the "productivity" of an economy grow faster than the supply of labor is growing, there will be a steady increase every decade in real wages for the workingman (assuming that the money supply is not expanded at a faster rate than goods and services are being produced, which brings on price inflation and either stagnant or lowered real wages). The means to insure such a faster growth of economic diversity and productivity is to provide a political environment that encourages *capital accumulation.* The way to accomplish this is to keep government bureaucratism and taxation at a minimal level.

This is why it is so ruinous to attempt to redistribute accumulated individual wealth in order to produce *equality* in society. When government confiscates such wealth through progressive taxation, that wealth is spent on "consumption" by massive bureaucracies and the special interest groups they support. This stifles the accumulation of capital, which decreases the growth of diversity and productivity. When the entrepreneurs who produce such wealth are allowed to retain it, it is spent on "investment" in new ideas and businesses. This increases the growth of diversity and productivity, which then creates higher wages and more profits for everybody. Government *dissipates* our wealth by directing it into channels of consumption; entrepreneurs *expand* our wealth by directing it into channels of investment.

This is a most vital point for Americans to grasp. We have been grievously misled throughout the 20th century by the liberal welfare philosophy that has preached the necessity of social and economic *equality* implemented through coercive redistribution of wealth programs. Only in this way, we have been told, can there be *justice*. Those who are better off must be forced to give up their affluence so that the poorer income groups can become better off.

But this conflicts with a most basic fact of reality: wealth is not static, i.e., a fixed amount that needs to be divided among a society's citizens. It is expansive and infinite — *ever growing* in direct proportion to the ideas and economic effort that are put forth by those citizens.

In order for wealth to be expansive, however, there has to be *adequate incentive* or there will be no wealth created at all for anybody. Progressive tax rates work against this process by stifling basic human motivation because they destroy each individual's incentive to produce. As a result, less and less overall wealth is created rather than more and more. The tide of prosperity is *lowered*, and with it both large and small boats. Society as a whole becomes worse off. The recent history of socialism verifies this more profoundly than any academic analysis. The Russian people are now bordering on Third World living standards because they bought into the Marxist myth.

So society does not need to be *equalized* in wealth and status in order for the poor to become better off. It merely needs to be *free*, and all individuals will become better off as a result of the wealth creation stemming from that freedom. Naturally, those who work the hardest and smartest will gain the most, but everyone will gain in direct proportion to their effort. If society's citizens are simply permitted to retain and *freely invest* their earnings, there is no limit to how high a tide they can create.

The View From the Left

The political left, of course, puts a decidedly different spin on this issue of growth and its effect upon wealth accumulation and distribution in society. In their eyes, *economic growth* is no longer a relevant factor in raising the standard of living for the lower classes.

Because of modern technology and the emergence of a global marketplace, they claim it is now impossible for the poor to improve themselves through economic growth alone. They cite recent statistics demonstrating the stagnation of real median family income during the past 20 years with the bottom half of the population getting a smaller slice of the total national income. The necessary medicine, they assert, is a dose of the old time religion: federal spending programs.

Here we have a classic case of the collectivist mind advocating government intervention into the market to solve problems that are the result of government intervention into the market. It is true that real median family income has barely budged since the early seventies. But this is not the fault of free enterprise; this is the fault of an obtuse government that has so regimented and punitively taxed its citizens that the entrepreneurial function and its *creation of capital* have been disastrously diminished. Unshackle the creative spirit of men from the ball and chain of Great Society bureaucratism, eliminate the onerous progressive tax system, stop the government from inflating the money supply, and real family income would begin to climb again as it has throughout our history as a nation.

Restore the standards and discipline to our schools that "progressive education" has destroyed, and the necessary skills for the lower half of the population to confront an ever changing world economy would once again be taught. Low wages result from low skills, from ignorance, and from inability to read and calculate. Under the guidance of liberal egalitarianism during the past 30 years, our schools have ceased to impart the basic necessities for even minimal growth of human minds.

Here then lie the sources of stagnating family income for Americans: confiscatory taxation which discourages incentive to earn and invest, excessive regulation of businesses which discourages entrepreneurship, central bank inflation of the money supply which discourages saving, and the utopian failures of progressive education which destroy basic skills. These are not problems that derive from free enterprise, but from *government intervention into free enterprise.*

It is incredible how intellectuals who have been shown to be 180 degrees wrong in their worldview will still tenaciously cling to that worldview. To the political left, socialism's dream of government mandated egalitarianism is still realizable. All that is needed are some theoretical adjustments. Never mind that the entire history of the world conflicts with their analysis. Never mind that rational economics refutes their theoretical models. Never mind that plain common sense screams out that men and women will not work hard if their economic endeavors are redistributed through centralized government and if their minds are left vacant because of educational rot. Still the political left persists in more of the same governmental poisons that stultify the primary requisite for social well being — *economic growth.*

Contrary to the neo-Marxist and neo-Keynesian thinking of today's academy, the power of economic growth is not something that goes out of date. It does not fade away because the world's economies are undergoing "profound structural change." The world's economies have always been undergoing "profound structural change." Economic growth's power to improve the lot of mankind is still a force today as it was yesterday, and as it will be tomorrow. There is no other force with which to prosper. And there are no other ways to ignite this force than through the efficiency, the incentive, and the knowledge that erupt from a free-market.

The political left has chosen to cling to the past in the hope that Marx was somehow not so catastrophically wrong after all — not unlike flat-earthers clinging to the Ptolemaic universe in the aftermath of the 16th century astronomers' new discoveries. Political leftists are busily at work churning out anti-growth propaganda tracts like their recent paean to Big Government, *America Unequal,* by Sheldon Danziger and Peter Gottshalk, which claims that economic growth is not a major factor in determining the relative wealth or poverty of a society. Just like rain, I suppose, is not a major factor in the verdancy and longevity of a forest.

Income Disparity and Wealth

What the political left needs to grasp is that a "laissez-faire" society that creates a GDP of $10 trillion annually, with *highly disparate* income levels between upper and lower classes, is far superior (morally and economically) to a "social welfare" society that creates a GDP of $3 trillion with *more equal* income levels. Drastically reducing the government will give us the former; continuing to increase government will bring us the latter.

What does it matter how much disparity there is between upper and lower class incomes if there is three times more wealth created for all levels? Why should we be concerned with corporate executives making $10-$20 million salaries in a capitalist economy when the *lower* classes of capitalism earn far more per capita than the *middle* classes of socialism?

Remember, wealth is not a fixed amount for society to divvy up. The economy of a free society is not a zero-sum game in which there must be a corresponding loser for every winner. Wealth is infinitely expansive. Free enterprise is a winning game for everyone who wishes to put forth effort. The stratospheric salaries paid to entrepreneurs and corporate executives are because these individuals have *created* something monumental and immensely productive. Through their "ideas" and "expertise," they have *increased the capital stock* of society in a dramatic way. This is why the market rewards them with such stratospheric incomes — because they have contributed ingeniously and spectacularly to the economic well being of mankind. This is the nature of a free-market; it pays the highest rewards to those individuals who produce the most for their fellow-man. Since *mental* energy contributes thousands of times more to the capital stock of a society than *physical* energy, the rewards will always be the greatest for those individuals who think creatively rather than labor routinely. Because the theoreticians of the left attempt to alter this natural order of the market through confiscatory taxation, they snuff out the creative *mental* energy that is necessary to increase the capital stock of society.

Without a grasp of this simple economic truth, one is forever doomed to a false view of social reality. It is because of the increase in society's capital stock that the laboring classes become capable of producing more and consequently earning more. Mammoth salaries paid to entrepreneurs and corporate executives do not *reduce* the earnings of workers. They *increase* the workers' earnings because they provide the necessary stimulus for creative *mental* energy to continually burst forth and expand the capital stock of society.

The incredible increases in wealth that the American worker has received this past century are the result of the American innovator. Left to fend for themselves in a "profitless" society, humans would continue to dig with crude shovels, travel in ox carts, write with quill and ink, and remain at a low output level. There would be sparse economic growth, few new ideas, *very little production per man hour*, and consequently *very low wages*. But unleash the entrepreneurial innovator in a free-market by allowing him to freely sell his ideas and services (and retain the profits therein), and that society's citizens will be given harvesters, automobiles, printing presses and computers with which to *increase their productivity* and enhance their lives. There will be a torrent of economic growth and increased wealth for everyone because there will be constant increases in overall capital.

When Marx exhorted the workers of the world to unite and seize the wealth of society's entrepreneurs, he was telling them to destroy society's capital stock. He was venting the voice of irrationality and power lust that has been responsible for the stagnant misery of all command societies throughout history—from the pharaohs of ancient Egypt, to the feudal aristocracies of the

Middle Ages, to the regimental horrors of Nazi Germany and Soviet Russia. As a result, the socialist left is now imprisoned in a paradigm that stultifies the very foundation of man's existence — his free creativity.

The American left counters that it does not endorse *pure* socialism and its abject poverty, but instead the more workable "social welfarism" of Sweden with per capita income levels that are comparable to the U.S., maintaining that we should be remade in the Scandinavian image. But Sweden suffers the same devastating problems of America at present, only in more accentuated form: inflation, punitive taxes, debilitating regulation, extravagant government spending, anemic growth, and a relentless shrinking of personal freedom. Sweden is merely LBJ's Great Society writ more extreme. Her people have become servile automatons whose lives are planned and guided for them by a smothering, omnipresent maze of government bureaucracies from cradle to grave.

While America's total tax bite (federal, state and local) consumes a devastating *40 percent* of the average upper-middle class income, Sweden's total tax bite takes *65 percent* of that income. The U.S. per capita tax burden in 1992 was $6,757 out of a median income of $24,850; Sweden's was $14,234.[16] With Sweden's way lies death for the American dream of individualism in favor of Huxley's Brave New World.

A horrifying glimpse into the reality of Sweden and its alleged social welfare ideal is *The New Totalitarians,* written during the seventies by the critically acclaimed journalist, Roland Huntford. Its message is that "social welfarism" merely brings us to a slave society more slowly and subtly than communism and fascism. But in the long run, central government control, with its redistribution of wealth and regimentation of individual businesses, will wipe out individual freedom.

Instead of the Orwellian boot stamping on the face of freedom that took place in Nazi Germany and Soviet Russia, social welfarism gives us an insufferable and manipulative Nanny State, whose politicians spew out election year cant about freedom and progress, while smuggling incessant tax increases and monetary inflation in the back door to fund the government's domination of our lives. Does it make any difference that social welfarists use corruption of the language and brainwashing of the media, rather than concentration camps and firing squads to build their mega-state? Like communism and fascism, social welfarism eventually stamps on the face of freedom. It just does so in a softer, more insidious manner by deluding the people, through demagoguery and tax progressivity, into voting away their freedom and their earnings.

That the political left can ignore such obvious economic and historical evolution, and continue to call for still more government bureaucracy and still more progressive tax rates, is a stark indicator of its pervasive philosophical bankruptcy.

Conservative Unreason

Sadly, it is not only the political left that has chosen to seek remedies from the specious policies of statism. There are now forces on the right proposing a New Mercantilism to protect jobs and counter stagnant income growth. In order to aid the working class of America, political columnist and presidential candidate Patrick Buchanan alleges we need a new protectionism of stiff tariffs to keep out "unfair" competition from foreign lands.

This is just another policy of unreason that sacrifices everyone's long run well-being for short run favors to inefficient corporations. A free-market requires men and women to endure both change and the possibility of being outproduced. This is the price people must pay to become prosperous as a society. The political left has always been reluctant to pay such a price, opting for a huge interventionist government to prohibit the "disruptive growth" that comes with a free economic order. But there are also reservoirs of such an animus among conservatives. The Big Government brand of conservative wishes to thwart the "creative destruction" of the marketplace by instituting controls on domestic firms and tariffs on foreign firms. In this way, he hopes to have the fruits of capitalism without its competitive rigors. It is a vain hope. Freedom has a price, and it is that companies rise and fall in accord with the demand of consumers and the quality of one's competition. Legally prohibiting such competition with controls will not create more jobs nor more wealth; it will create economic stasis.

Trade protectionism overlooks the fact that *less than 3 percent* of our GDP comes from imports of low-wage economies. To erect a wall of tariffs around America might protect a small percentage of jobs, but at the cost of higher consumer prices and a loss of dynamism in the market. A *free*-market will always create more jobs than it loses because it is wealth expanding.

Hong Kong's economy off the coast of China is an excellent, thriving example to prove the validity of this. As Milton Friedman points out in an article for the *Wall Street Journal*, after World War II, Hong Kong opted for economic freedom while its mother country, Great Britain, moved toward socialism. The results of the next four decades could not be more telling. Hong Kong has no significant natural resources, it had a severe refugee problem, and it suffered a rapidly growing population.

"Under these adverse circumstances," writes Friedman, "the salvation of Hong Kong has been its complete free trade and free market policy. No tariffs on imports, no subsidies or other privileges to exports. (The only restrictions are those that Hong Kong has been forced to impose by pressure from other countries, including the U.S., as under the multifiber agreement.) There is no fixing of prices or wages; few if any restrictions on entry into business or trade; and government spending and taxes have been kept low. The top tax rate on personal income is 25%, with a maximum average rate of 15%....

"By 1960, per capita gross domestic product (in 1995 prices) was $2,247, less than one-third Britain's $7,906. By 1994, the situation had dramatically reversed. Per-capita GDP in Hong Kong had multiplied nearly eight-fold to $17,832, and was one-third higher than Britain's $13,430....

"[W]hat a striking demonstration of how much better free trade and free markets are for the ordinary citizen than the protectionism of Mr. Buchanan and the 'fair trade' of President Clinton. 'Fair' is in the eye of the beholder; free is the verdict of the market." [17]

The difference between Britain and Hong Kong during the past 40 years is the difference between debilitating sclerosis and productive dynamism. America's choice could not be more clear.

A Lesson for Modern America

Regrettably, there will always be a sizeable number of complaints in a free society from those who feel they are not earning enough or don't feel secure enough. This is the nature of life and of humans. But a dangerously acute problem has evolved in the past 50 years because the socialist trend of the 20th century has led us to a view of government in which everyone's complaints about the vicissitudes of life should be turned over to the political system for redress. By passing legislation, Washington is to somehow ameliorate everyone's problems and produce a utopia of unbounded plenty and security where no needs go unfulfilled, no fears unallayed.

In the previous century, a man's problems were his own, his family's, his church's, and his community's. Washington had next to nothing to do with the lives of American citizens. This has all dramatically changed during our present century, however. With the enactment of the income tax (along with institution of the Federal Reserve) in 1913, a massive *politicization* of human life was made possible. The Federal Government now intervenes into the most minute affairs of everyone, and it does so because men and women have lost the *pride of independence* that is necessary for a free-market society to function. Americans have ceased to be pioneers, stalwart, strong-willed, self-reliant.

Calls for wealth redistribution and protectionist trade policies are rooted in this drift away from independence and in the longing for a life of *total security* that entails no risk, no need to compete, no need to move locations and retrain, no need to innovate and change one's thinking. Such policy proposals are not in the spirit of America, and they are not compatible with a free-market way of life. A free society does not owe its citizens a living nor an equal level of income with their fellows.

A free-market economy is not perfect because human beings are not perfect and much of life is inscrutable. But if we have learned anything during this past century, it is that men and women can improve the conditions of their lives immensely if they are allowed to *grow,* to interact mind and money in the absence of coercion from government.

The fact that there will always be a wide disparity of income levels in a free-market society does not mean the free-market is unjust. It means men and women are possessed of different levels of intelligence, energy and ambition in their approaches to life. Therefore, they will earn vastly different sums of wealth in their lives. Such disparate wealth levels are not wrong as long as the economy has the potential to expand and low income earners have the opportunity to *raise themselves* through work and saving. Because of its protection of property and its provision of equal rights, capitalism offers more of such potential and opportunity than any system that has ever been devised or ever will be devised. The only injustice is government policy aimed at suppressing such opportunity and potential.

The simple economic lesson that we must glean from all of this is: Because the rich do not sock their wealth away in tin cans in their backyards, because they put it to work "serving their fellow-man," there takes place an explosive creation of opportunities, jobs, ideas, technologies and growth, which in turn creates lower-cost goods and services plus ever rising real wages and profits for all who wish to work hard. Wealth begets wealth if it is left in the hands of the people and not confiscated to shore up slothful government bureaucracies.

Here lies the major flaw of the federal income tax, however. It violates the *equal rights* of Americans in order to mandate *equal conditions* throughout society, and in the process destroys prosperity and justice for all. It allows government to expropriate ever larger portions of our earnings and spend them for us. As a result, our earnings are now consumed by swarms of special interest groups instead of being invested in capital accumulating ventures.

Increased Revenue Requires Rational Policy

The second erroneous principle undergirding the income tax is a point discussed at length by prominent tax expert Daniel J. Pilla in his book, *How To Fire The IRS.* It is the assumption that increased revenue for the government can be obtained by taxing people's profits and productivity. This, too, conflicts with the basic laws of economics and capital accumulation. In attempting to raise its revenue by progressively taxing profits and productivity, the Federal Government greatly reduces the amount of money that Americans can save and invest. In other words, it decreases the "accumulation of capital," which causes the nation's productivity to slow to a sluggish pace. This then deleteriously affects the government's potential for revenues.

Remember it is only out of personal savings that investment in new ideas and businesses will take place, and it is only out of such investment that a rising standard of living can be achieved. Because the progressive income tax consumes savings and profits, it decreases economic growth and prosperity. Thus, it *decreases the tax base* and the resulting revenues for government which then requires higher and higher tax rates to make up the difference.

As Pilla repeatedly reminds us, "What you tax, you get less of. What you subsidize, you get more of."[18] By taxing income, we get *less* savings, investment, growth and prosperity.

Laurence J. Kotlikoff, professor of economics at Boston University, maintains that our national savings rate is at a disastrous level. In a recent Cato Institute Policy Analysis, he states that we saved only 1.7 percent of net domestic product in 1991, the lowest in the post World War II period. As comparison, we saved 9.1 percent of net domestic product from 1950 to 1970, and 8.5 percent from 1970 through 1980.[19]

The primary reason for this dearth of savings is the complexity and the punitive nature of our income, corporate, capital gains and estate taxes which have slowly become entrenched over the past 40 years. The *Tax Reform Act of 1986* was the final straw on the camel's back of our system. Changes in depreciation schedules, deduction for capital losses, and long term capital gains were enacted that further reduced the entrepreneur's ability to accumulate capital in the marketplace. The combination of these three changes, on top of all the redistributive decrees of past decades, has had a very damaging effect upon America's rate of *capital investment*. When we factor in the ever-rising FICA taxes for small businesses and the ever-increasing complexity of the IRS code, the adverse effect on savings and investment is devastating. In the 1990's, our investment rate has averaged 3.8 percent. In the sixties, it averaged 10.5 percent.[20] With a proper tax policy (on consumption instead of income), it could be raised to the 15 percent range.

The answer to all this is clear: we need more than just a restoration of pre-1986 conditions. We must abolish the grossly inefficient income, corporation, capital gains, estate and gift taxes altogether, replacing them with a simple tax on *consumption* — i.e., a national sales tax. In this way, billions of dollars would be released into the channels of economic entrepreneurship and production, thereby increasing in a revolutionary way the well-being of Americans at all income levels.

"Close your eyes and imagine for a moment an America without an income tax," writes Stephen Moore of Cato Institute in a recent *National Review* article. "April 15 is no longer a day of dread. The federal tax on personal income, corporate income, and capital gains is zero. Estate and gift taxes have been abolished. The most intrusive institution in America, the Internal Revenue Service, has been shut down and its 115,000 auditors and enforcement agents have been disbanded. All federal revenues are collected through a national sales tax, and it is no longer the government's business how much money you make and what you do with it once you earn it. H&R Block has gone into Chapter 11; tens of thousands of tax accountants, attorneys, and lobbyists are finding new professions; and now even drug lords pay their taxes.

"That giant sucking sound you're hearing is investment capital from all over the globe pouring into the world's newest tax haven: the United States. Freed from the shackles of an anti-work, anti-investment, anti-saving tax system, America surges ahead of Japan, Germany, and the rest of Europe in economic growth." [21]

The above scenario could be a reality in our lives tomorrow if the American people will only rise up to resist the sophistry and demagoguery that our liberal Beltway elites spew out during election time to try and polarize us with class envy and confusion. Radical tax reform is gaining a larger and larger following as each month goes by. The political establishment and its "special interest controlled" tax system are beginning to crack. All that is necessary for our success is a fervent political ground swell at the grassroots level. Once the American people are armed with the true facts of this issue, then Washington's social engineers and their game of "tax and spend" are finished. They are finished because their vision is at cross purposes with the great American experiment in freedom. They are finished because reason, fairness, simplicity, morality, prosperity and constitutionality all lie with our cause.

Income Tax Compliance Costs

In addition to the constitutional, philosophical and complexity problems of the federal income tax noted above, there exists yet another egregious flaw in the operation of such a tax. This is what economists call its *compliance cost*, i.e., what it costs in actual dollar figures for the nation as a whole to put up with and implement the income tax.

Daniel Pilla asks in *How To Fire The IRS,* "What is the cost to the American economy of dealing with the tax law, understanding the changes, keeping records, supplying information, filing returns, hiring professionals, handling audits, challenging penalties and computer notices, coping with collection, and just generally suffering under the agency's enforcement thumb? The IRS and Congress seem oblivious to these costs but they are real and quantifiable." [22]

Pilla then refers to research economist James L. Payne's *Costly Returns: The Burdens of the U.S. Tax System.* In this all-inclusive study, Payne analyzed the vast array of compliance costs for the income tax. He researched "the enforcement costs of audits and appeals, the costs of tax litigation and enforced collection, the economic disincentive costs, the costs of tax evasion and avoidance," the underground economy, and the administration costs government incurs in maintaining the system. Payne's shocking conclusion was that the cost for society to operate and abide by our present income tax laws is as much as 65 percent of whatever revenues are obtained. [23]

This means that for every dollar the American citizen pays to the Federal Government in taxes, it costs society 65 cents to pay it. We, as a nation, paid $639 billion in direct taxes on income in 1993. This means it cost us *$415 billion* to maintain government by these taxes. Is it any wonder that our economy is creeping along like a giant socialistic turtle?

In 1990, American individuals and businesses spent a total of 5.4 billion man hours figuring out, complying with, and filing their tax forms. As a result of all this nonsensical complexity, more and more Americans are having to resort to paid professional accountants and tax preparers with each passing year. Seeing that our compliance costs are 65 cents for every $1.00 collected and headed even higher in the future, a more irrational, Byzantine system could hardly be imagined. In light of these facts, it should be obvious that America needs to take *radical action* on this issue — not just tinker around with "flattening out the rates."

It should be pointed out here that a national sales tax would cost us as individuals close to *zero dollars* in compliance costs. This is because the state governments already collect state sales taxes. The collection procedures are already in place, and they can be used as the mechanism to collect a national sales tax also. It will cost no more for states to collect their present 7 percent sales tax plus a 16 percent NST than to collect the 7 percent sales tax alone. The state collection agencies need merely add the new rate onto the old rate. Compliance costs are not increased in any significant way.

In his book, Pilla advocates that the national sales tax not be collected by any agency of the Federal Government. It should be "collected by the *states* alone," then turned over to the U.S. Treasury "pursuant to regulations established for that purpose." In this way, the national Treasury will have no claim to audit or investigate individuals and businesses. They will be required to direct any and all enforcement procedures to the *"state governments only."* An effective shield between the individual and Washington's Leviathan will thus be erected. [24]

The NST is Not a VAT

It is very important to understand that the national sales tax is not a Value Added Tax (VAT). The VAT is a tax that is common in Europe. It is like a sales tax, and it is being proposed by many Big Government supporters in Washington as the "tax of the 21st century."

The VAT is a tax on the *increase in the value* that businesses add to a product as it proceeds through the manufacturing to retailing chain. It works like a sales tax except for two differences: 1) it is charged on all levels of the market process — raw materials production, manufacturing of finished goods, wholesale distribution, retail sales, etc. — instead of just at the retail level; and 2) it is not charged on the total price of the good but instead only on the value added to it by the seller.

For example, in the manufacturing and processing of a loaf of bread, there are several stages that different materials go through before the finished product emerges. In the first stage, wheat is grown, harvested and sold to a flour mill. Let's say that the amount of wheat for one loaf of bread originally costs the farmer 3 cents in seed, which he sells after harvesting to the flour mill for 13 cents. Under a 10 percent VAT, the farmer must charge a *1 cent VAT* to the mill for that wheat because he has added 10 cents of value to the wheat from planting to harvesting. The price charged the flour mill is thus 14 cents.

In the second stage, the mill takes the harvested wheat and grinds it into flour, then packages and sells it for 34 cents to a bakery. The value added to the wheat by the mill is 20 cents. Thus it charges a *2 cent VAT* to the bakery, bringing the total cost of the flour to 36 cents.

In the third stage, the bakery takes the flour and mixes it with other ingredients worth 20 cents to produce a loaf of bread, which it sells to the supermarket for $1.16. The value it has added to the flour and other ingredients is 60 cents. Thus it charges a *6 cent VAT* to the supermarket, bringing the total cost of the loaf of bread to $1.22.

In the fourth stage, the supermarket then puts the bread on the shelf at $1.85 for the retail-buying public and charges a *6 cent VAT* because it has increased the value of the bread by 63 cents. Total cost of the bread to the consumer is $1.91, which includes a total of 15 cents in VAT charges.

Each stage of production along the way has *added value* to the previous stage, and a tax is charged according to the amount of that value. Since at each stage a tax is charged only on the amount of the added value and not the entire selling price, you avoid the problem of "cascading" where taxes are charged on top of taxes all along the way.

There are two major problems with this form of taxation: 1) It gets extremely complex when all the various production levels begin to calculate their particular value added. The above example of bread is very simplified. Pilla reveals in *How To Fire The IRS* that in the production and distribution of a book, from lumber harvested in the forest to printed tome in Dalton's, there can be as many as seven stages of transactions which often intertwine and can even assume each other's roles. It gets quite complicated.

The compliance burden for the VAT soon brings a heavy load of paperwork to all the business transactions, the hiring of labor, and the purchasing of materials and services that go into extracting, manufacturing, distributing and retailing marketable goods to the public. "Value added" is subject to *interpretation* by whoever is wielding the calculator. All kinds of statistical nuances, subtleties and temptations begin to enter into the monthly course of business. The government authorities collecting such taxes end up becoming extremely intrusive in order to extract their "rightful due." Rates invariably get raised to compensate for lost revenue due to compliance problems. The whole system invariably evolves into an arbitrary and convoluted torture chamber of computations.

2) A second problem with the VAT is that it can be *easily raised* by an ambitious government and remain hidden from the great majority of the voting public. When the VAT is raised on the price of flour, for example, the only ones aware of the tax are the businesses that sell and purchase flour. The voting public remains unaware. All they know is that the price of bread went up. They blame the supermarkets, however, while the politicians reap a nice

bump in their revenues. This is not a healthy economic or political condition to establish. Taxes, in order to be just and workable, need to be open and recognizable for what they are and where they come from. In this way the political authorities instituting them can be held accountable. Value Added Taxes do not allow for such openness and accountability.

The reader should now see that there is a distinct difference between a national sales tax and a VAT. The NST will be very *visible* and very *simple*. Unlike a VAT, it cannot be hidden in the intricate stages of production and distribution that comprise the long chain of getting raw materials into finished goods to sell in retail stores. The NST is a onetime, flat tax on the total sales price charged to the buying public on all *final use* goods and services. There is no interpretation of "added value." There is no complexity. And, most importantly, the politicians who enact such a tax will be held accountable for it before the voters.

America needs definite reform and new policy ideas in the political arena, but she most certainly *does not need a VAT.* The collectivist establishment is busy floating trial balloons in an attempt to convince the public as to the necessity of passing legislation for a federal Value Added Tax. Such a tax must be rejected by all freedom loving Americans. The VAT is a nightmare for industrious citizens and a hidden source of revenue for disingenuous politicians. America needs a VAT like she needs another Jimmy Carter administration.

Is the NST Regressive?

This is the major rap against the national sales tax. Most academic and media pundits in America claim that any type of consumption based taxation is *regressive* (i.e., it hits the lower classes harder than it hits the upper classes). This, as we will see, is a misperception.

In order to understand this issue better, however, we must first review the *three* different kinds of taxes. Big Government advocates always convey this issue in terms of two kinds only: progressive and regressive. In other words, all taxes supposedly fall into one or the other of these two categories. And since regressive is definitely unjust, we must utilize a progressive taxation system. It is the only equitable means of revenue for government. To such intellects, any tax that is not progressive is therefore automatically regressive, and therefore not permissible in a humane society. But this is a fallacy. There is a *third* choice that establishment authorities, through either ignorance or deception, leave out of their analyses. The third choice is a "uniform" tax (or as some term it, a proportional tax). This is a most important point: there are not two but three fundamental kinds of taxes — regressive, progressive and uniform.

1) A *regressive* tax is where people pay a higher percentage the *less* they earn or consume. Let's say we taxed every one of the 125 million working people in America $5,000 each. That would raise approximately $625 billion in revenue, but it would be extremely unfair. The individual making $15,000 per year would be in the 33 percent tax bracket while the individual making $150,000 per year would be in the 3 percent bracket.

2) A *progressive* tax is where people pay a higher percentage the *more* they earn or consume, which is the method we employ at present with the federal income tax. An individual who earns $15,000 per year is taxed at approximately 9 percent of that $15,000, while an individual who earns $150,000 per year is taxed at approximately 30 percent of his gross income. (These figures are for single payers taking the standard deduction for themselves.)

3) A *uniform* tax is where everyone pays the *same percentage* no matter what their income or consumption is. The rate is not altered according to who you are, or what you earn, or what you buy. All men and women pay the same rate, i.e., the same propor-

tion of their income or consumption. If someone earns or consumes $15,000, they are taxed at 16 percent, and if they earn or consume $150,000, they are also taxed at 16 percent.

All three of these forms of taxation have been used at different times throughout history, but which one is the fairest method when considered within the context of the American principle of "equal rights under the law?" Under our present progressive tax system (when federal, state, city and FICA taxes are factored in), we are allowing some men the right to 92 percent disposal of their income while allowing others the right to only 50 percent disposal of their income. In other words, we are taking *different* proportions of men's property depending upon what class they are in — lower, middle or upper. Thus, we are applying the law *differently* to men who are supposed to be equal before the law. To paraphrase the late Benjamin Rogge, the blindfolded Goddess of Justice has been allowed to peek. "Tell me first who you are and what you earn," she says, "then I will tell you how the tax laws apply to you." This is privilege and arbitrary law, the harbingers of every tyranny throughout history.

If it is wrong for the less productive people to be penalized by a higher rate under a regressive tax, then it is also wrong for the more productive people to be penalized by a higher rate under a progressive tax. Since a "uniform" tax is the only method that allows all men and women the right to the *same proportion* of their property, is it not the only method compatible with *equal rights?* Is it not then the only method of taxation compatible with *justice?*

The national sales tax becomes regressive only if one's taxes paid are compared to one's income earned. For example, a man making $15,000 per year, who consumes $13,000, would pay $2,080 under an NST of 16 percent. A man making $150,000 per year, who consumes $100,000, would pay $16,000. When their "consumption" is used as the standard, they both are paying a uniform rate of 16 percent. But if we switch to "income" as the standard, then the low earner pays 14 percent ($2,080 divided by his income of $15,000 = 14 percent), while the high earner pays only 11 percent ($16,000 divided by his income of $150,000 = 11 percent). This makes the tax higher for the low income earner, and thus *regressive.*

This is not proper computation, however. Why should a consumption tax use "income" as its standard? The NST, being a consumption tax, should use consumption as its standard. If this is done, then the NST is neither a regressive nor a progressive tax; it is a *uniform* or *proportional* tax. In other words, since the rate is uniform, one's taxes are in proportion to one's consumption level. Because the rich consume much more than the poor, they will thus pay much higher dollar amounts of taxes even though the tax rate is the same for everyone.

To understand this issue of standards better, let's reverse its components. Would we judge an income tax by using "consumption" as the standard? For example, if a man makes $50,000 in today's society, he pays approximately $11,000 in taxes or a 22 percent rate. Would it be fair to say that since he consumes $25,000, he actually pays a 44 percent income tax rate ($11,000 divided by $25,000 = 44 percent)? Of course not. To compute a proper rate and judge its fairness, we must use income as the standard for income tax rates and consumption as the standard for consumption tax rates.

So, the national sales tax is *not* a regressive tax that affects the poor unjustly. As further assurance of this, all Congress needs to do is present NST legislation that excludes expenditures on food and housing for all Americans. This keeps the tax rate relatively uniform and proportional for everyone, yet structures it so that it doesn't come down in a heavy manner upon the lower income classes. Since these classes spend a large percentage of their income on food and housing, their tax burden ends up no greater than middle and upper class citizens.

For example, single wage earners making $13,000 annually would pay *less* taxes under the NST than they do under our present income tax system. After the standard deduction of $6,400, they pay *$994 in income taxes* under our present code. Under the NST, however, single wage earners making $13,000 (who spend $3,000 a year on food and $4,200 a year on housing) would have only $5,800 that would be taxed. If they saved nothing and consumed the entire $5,800, they would pay *$928 in sales taxes* under a 16 percent NST.

So the NST is *not* "massively regressive" as the Washington establishment and the media declare. It is proportional and fair, and it will result in low income earners paying *$66 less* in taxes than they presently pay.

Flat Tax Flaws

As any observer of the congressional scene knows, the national sales tax is being debated in political circles today along with several other proposals to "reform" the tax system. One of those other proposals is the so called *flat tax,* whereby one set rate of 17 percent would raise as much money as our present progressive system with multiple brackets of 15 percent to 39 percent. Such a flat tax is not without merit, for it would greatly simplify the present mess that masquerades as a fair system. But profound weaknesses exist in the flat tax that Americans need to be made aware of.

There are three flaws in all the flat tax proposals: 1) They do not get rid of the IRS and its egregious harassment. 2) They *increase* progressivity rather than *reduce* it, so they are not "flat" taxes. And 3) they must give subtle breaks to the rich in order to be growth enhancing. Let's investigate each of these flaws.

IRS Accommodation

Most important of all, flat tax proposals do not get rid of the IRS. This arrogant, intrusive agency will still be operational, and it will continue all of its unconstitutional policies. The poor, beleaguered taxpayer will still be considered guilty until proven innocent. He will still have his bank accounts subject to seizure, his property subject to liens, his records and his privacy subject to surveillance. He will still have his business affairs, purchases and profits subject to agonizing regulations and record keeping. He will still have to endure audits, penalties, appeals, forms, schedules — the entire litany of arbitrary bureaucratic enforcement procedures that constitutes IRS methodology.

True, there will be no need to audit taxpayers on the question of "deductions." The simplicity of the flat tax does solve that problem. But businesses will still be plagued with it, and the IRS will still be looming over everyone and snooping into their records to verify their *declared income*.

Having been released from the job of overseeing the deductions of American taxpayers, the IRS will merely have that much more time and desire to apply to other aspects of our financial affairs. They will use such time to increase audits, surveillances and seizures. Thus, the flat tax will not decrease IRS intrusion into our lives; it will unleash the IRS to continue its intimidatory ways.

The IRS presently audits about 3 percent of the 118 million tax-payer returns it receives every year. This is because it has neither the time nor the manpower to properly audit any more than this. But with much of the yoke of "deductions policing" removed from its duties, it *will* have the time and manpower. Does anyone believe that the IRS will suddenly reduce its staff because the flat tax has reduced its deductions monitoring requirements. Hardly. The IRS is an authoritarian bureaucracy, and it will merely seek other areas to snoop into and oversee our lives — undoubtedly by expanding its efforts into further harassing the business community (especially small businessmen and self-employed taxpayers). Life will be unmitigated hell for these groups under the flat tax. Audits will not decrease; they will expand by whopping percentages to verify those returns in which declared income is computed by taxpayers or their accountants.

Pilla points out in his book that in 1992 Americans filed over 43 million Short Forms (the 1040A), claiming income of under $25,000. These taxpayers claimed *no itemized deductions* other than their IRA's. Yet the IRS audited 300,480 of these returns and found only 12.5 percent of them to be in the clear. The 87.5 percent declared by the IRS to owe more were assessed an average of $2,599 in addition to taxes they had paid. [25]

In *Why You Can't Trust The IRS,* a 1995 Policy Analysis for Cato Institute, Pilla reports that every year the IRS appears before Congress to solicit more money and more discretionary powers, more computerization capacity and more agents with which to investigate, audit, penalize (and thus terrorize) the American public. And every year Congress complies with the IRS' demands to increase its enforcement procedures.

The IRS, he reveals, announced on December 20, 1994, an all pervasive plan to link its computer systems with every public and private database throughout the country in order to obtain "on-line access" to American citizens' business, financial and commercial activities. The agency intends to construct electronic dossiers on all Americans, which will give it a chilling and ominous power to spy on every individual in the nation. [26]

As Senator Richard Lugar pointed out in his 1996 campaign for the presidency, new IRS plans also include what they call "lifestyle audits," which are meant to determine whether or not we are living beyond our means. Under such an audit, IRS agents will come out and evaluate our home and neighborhood, our education, our personal associates, our cultural and family ties, our children's habits and activities, what vacations we take, what clothing and jewelry we wear, what restaurants we eat in. They will interview our neighbors, business associates, co-workers and fellow family members to procure information about how we conduct our lives.

Does this look like an institution that will *reduce* its intrusiveness with the inception of a flat tax?

James Bovard tells us in *Lost Rights* that the IRS, in desperate straits to feed the bureaucracies of an out-of-control Federal Government, has declared virtual war on the business community. Its officials now encourage private companies to secretly betray their competitors; it seeks out snitches everywhere; and it now has the right to lie to Congress. Since 1954, the number of penalties the IRS can impose on taxpayers has shot from 13 to over 150. The IRS slammed over 33 million penalties on Americans in 1992. The amount of those penalties has climbed from $1.3 billion in 1978 to 12.5 billion in 1992. Yet, in 1990, almost half of the over 30 million penalty notices the IRS sent out to helpless taxpayers *were wrong!* The IRS wrongfully collected almost $7 billion in penalties in 1989. IRS agents seize over 10,000 homes, cars and pieces of property yearly from the American people. Bank account seizures have quadrupled since 1980. Liens are up over 200 percent since 1980, totaling 1.4 million yearly. The IRS has long rewarded its most aggressive agents according to the dollar amount of property they confiscate from taxpayers. IRS managers routinely pressure employees to make more seizures so that they can merit bonuses. In San Francisco, one IRS office had the following notice on its bulletin board: "Seizure fever. Catch it." [27]

This is not an institution that we as Americans can live with and reform. It is an institution that needs to be dismantled. But this will not take place under a flat tax. On the contrary, all the ugliest and most oppressive IRS policies will be expanded. All the emotional hassle of audits, all the time, expense and mental anguish of income and profit verification for both individuals and businesses, will remain under a flat tax.

The IRS is a malevolent organization, operating above the law, that blatantly contradicts the vision and meaning of America. It is inconceivable that our congressional leaders have allowed it to mushroom into the Orwellian monstrosity it is today. Helping now to promote its propaganda and continuance will bring neither freedom nor prosperity; it will only exacerbate the decadent trends of despotism in which we are embroiled.

The Flat Tax is Not Flat

The second glaring flaw in the flat tax proposals is that they do not reduce progressivity. Take for example Representative Dick Armey's call for a 17 percent flat tax. It provides for an $11,350 deduction for every adult and a $5,300 deduction for every child. This means that a family of four making $33,300 per year would not be taxed at all. Those families earning $40,000 would have only $6,700 in taxable income. Their taxes would be only $1,139, which is only 2.8 percent when computed as a percentage of their $40,000 earnings. This is what is called their "effective" or "true" rate. Then, as we go up the bracket ladder, the rates rise sharply:

```
$  40,000 income-$33,300 =   $ 6,700 x .17= $ 1,139 in taxes  (2.8%)
$  50,000 income-$33,300 =   $ 16,700 x .17= $ 2,839 in taxes  (5.7%)
$  60,000 income-$33,300 =   $ 26,700 x .17= $ 4,539 in taxes  (7.6%)
$  70,000 income-$33,300 =   $ 36,700 x .17= $ 6,239 in taxes  (8.9%)
$  80,000 income-$33,300 =   $ 46,700 x .17= $ 7,939 in taxes  (9.9%)
$100,000 income-$33,300 =   $ 66,700 x .17= $11,399 in taxes (11.3%)
$150,000 income-$33,300 = $ 116,700 x .17= $19,839 in taxes (13.2%)
$300,000 income-$33,300 = $ 266,700 x .17= $45,339 in taxes (15.1%)
$400,000 income-$33,300 = $ 366,700 x .17= $62,339 in taxes (15.6%)
$500,000 income-$33,300 = $ 466,700 x .17= $79,339 in taxes (15.9%)
```

This is not a flat tax; it is a *highly progressive* tax structure with rates that range from 0 to 16 percent depending on where a family of four falls on the earning scale between $33,300 and $500,000 annually.

Notice that the 0 to 16 percent rates actually contain more progressivity than our present 15 to 39 percent system does. The rate range is lower because the base is higher, but the progressivity is steeper. A $400,000 income earner who makes *ten* times what a $40,000 income earner does, would pay *fifty-five* times as much taxes under Armey-Shelby. Under our present system, he pays *twenty-one* times as much.

Notice also that all that is necessary to make a so-called flat tax into a progressive tax is to give everyone a personal deduction. The higher the deduction, the steeper it will make the progressivity of the rates. In this instance, the deductions are quite substantial ($11,350 for adults and $5,300 for every child), and thus, the rates become quite progressive. There is nothing to prohibit Congress from continually raising these deductions over the years, and thus making this "flat" tax even more progressive. In other words, more and more people can be put into the *zero percent category* by merely raising the deductions. What are the chances of Congress avoiding this temptation when it means they will receive more votes for doing so?

Therefore, one thing needs to be made very clear. Our taxes are certainly not being made *uniform* (i.e., more just) with the Armey-Shelby "flat" tax. This plan, as with others such as the Forbes plan and the Kemp guidelines, are basically just attempts at "tinkering around the edges" of a corrupt, inefficient and unconstitutional system. They are quintessential examples of the type of government "reform" that politicians love to present to the public because it doesn't genuinely change any fundamentals. These flat tax plans are Edsels; they do not get rid of the IRS, and they contain *more progressivity* than our present system does.

Families with two children earning $33,300 annually would be *tax exempt* under Armey-Shelby; yet they comprise a very large constituency of voters in this nation. And, of course, what about the families with three children who make $38,600, and the families with four children who make $43,900, and the families with four children and an elderly grandmother who make $49,200? What about the families with one child making $28,000, and a man and wife alone making $22,700, and all the single people making $11,350 per year? These people comprise probably 30 to 35 percent of the nation's voters, yet they would pay *zero taxes* and would therefore get Washington's present level of services and handouts totally free.

Thus, there would be absolutely no incentive for them to vote to reduce government spending on such services and handouts. Why should there be? Such services are being paid for by all those who make more money than they do. Thirty-five percent of the nation's voters would be *automatic supporters* of Big Government spending programs.

It is this policy of passing on the cost of government services to those in higher income groups that has been responsible for building the Leviathan over the past 50 years. The liberal vanguard of FDR and LBJ created a tax system in which huge numbers of voters pay *nothing* or *next to nothing* in taxes. Such voters are now in the hip pocket of the Academy-Bureaucracy-Media triad that is gradually collectivizing the American system. The flat tax would expand this captive constituency to even greater numbers.

I have great respect for Dick Armey and his conservative cohorts in Congress. Their desires for America are certainly pointing in the right direction. But this is hardly the way to *reduce* government.

The recent Kemp Tax Commission offers no improvement either. It urges major reform of the system in order to bring about more fairness, but then it puts forth the same flawed progressivity as Armey-Shelby.

In *Unleashing America's Potential*, the Kemp Commission states: "For taxable income above the personal exemption, if one taxpayer earns ten times as much as his neighbor, he should pay ten times as much in taxes. Not twenty times as much — as he would with multiple and confiscatory tax rates. Not five times as much — as he might with special loopholes. Ten times as much income, ten times as much taxes: That's the deal." [28]

The fly in the above ointment is the phrase, "For taxable income *above* the personal exemption." What good does it do to flatten out the rates *above* the personal exemption if we have created such heavy exemptions that the overall structure remains highly progressive?

A system where an individual earns *ten* times as much as his neighbor and pays *fifty-five* times as much taxes can hardly be said to be fair. Yet that is what takes place under the Armey plan, and Kemp's model would be similar. Those earning $400,000 pay $62,339; those earning $40,000 pay $1,139.

It is the overall structure's flatness or progressivity that is important, and which will acutely affect the voting preferences of the nation's citizens — not just the segment *above* personal exemptions. If the overall structure is progressive, then nothing has improved. Under the Armey and Kemp tax plans, not only will nothing have improved, it will have gotten *worse*. This will create no motivation whatsoever for the American people to reduce the gargantuan power of government in their lives.

If we are to reduce the level of government spending and intrusion in this country, then the burden of that spending and intrusion must be felt proportionately by *everyone*. Only in this way is there an incentive to vote for less of it.

For example, under a 16 percent national sales tax plan that exempts food and housing, a husband and wife who earn $22,700 annually (and pay $12,000 for food and housing and save $700) would pay the 16 percent levy on their remaining $10,000 of consumption. Thus, since they would have to pay $1,600 to the government to run Health and Human Services, HUD, the Energy and Education Departments, the EPA and OSHA, etc., there is a much better chance that they are going to favor elimination of such bureaucratic dinosaurs than if they pay *zero taxes* (as they do under Armey-Shelby). When election time rolls around, they are most likely going to want to phase out all unnecessary expenditures because that is the only way they are going to get their $1,600 in sales taxes lowered. They are going to want to reduce the federal welfare state rather than maintain it. Their $1,600 in consumption taxes is not enough to create an unbearable hardship in their lives, but it is enough of a bite to make them rethink their desire to continue voting for massive federal programs. They will realize that if those programs were reduced, then their taxes could be reduced. A 16 percent bite could become a 10 percent bite, and eventually even a 7 percent bite.

In this way, all able-bodied men and women would be helping to pull the wagon of economic endeavor rather than riding in the wagon, as traditional conservative wisdom has reminded us over the decades. All men and women would have a far more equal right to the property they produce. And all men and women would have an incentive to *reduce* government rather than *expand* it.

Our country is in a crisis of immense proportions because we have been playing the "income redistribution" game from Washington for over 50 years in an attempt to obtain government services at the expense of someone else. The time has come to end the game. This can best be done through a national sales tax in which all people pay as close to a *uniform rate* as possible, i.e., a sum proportional to their level of consumption on all goods and services other than food and housing.

By exempting food (for off-premise consumption) and housing (both owned and rented) from taxation under an NST, a slightly progressive structure is actually created, but it is far less progressive than our present system and certainly far less than the 0 to 16 percent or 0 to 19 percent systems that the Armey-Shelby and Kemp Commission plans would give us.

For example, if a man earns $11,350 under Armey's flat tax, he would pay zero taxes because everyone's first $11,350 in income is exempted. But under the national sales tax proposed here, if he consumes $11,350, only his food and housing concerns would be exempted. He, therefore, would pay a sales tax on all other consumption expenditures. Let's say he spends $3,000 on groceries and $4,200 on housing for the year, leaving $4,150 to be consumed elsewhere and taxed at 16 percent. This means he would pay $664 in sales taxes. Since he actually consumed $11,350 for the year, his effective rate is *6 percent*. (Please note: He pays $746 in income taxes under our present system. So, he saves $82 under an NST.)

On the high end of the spectrum is the man who earns $500,000 and spends $50,000 on food and housing while saving $150,000, leaving $300,000 to be taxed at 16 percent. This means he would pay $48,000 in sales taxes. Since he actually consumed $350,000 during the year, his effective tax rate is *14 percent*.

Thus, under an NST we would have a system where the true rates range from 6 to 14 percent, while with the flat tax the true rates range from 0 to 16 percent under Armey-Shelby and probably 0 to 19 percent under a Kemp plan. Under the NST, everyone in society would *pay something* in taxes. This is a far healthier system for the country, and a far more just system for the individual. I realize that such reasoning will not appeal to those of statist inclination. Nevertheless, the lack of uniform tax rates, more than any other factor in the political-economic arena, lies behind the explosive growth of our government. The more *uniformity* we can build into our tax system, the more control we will have over government expansion.

The reader should now see that the primary cause of government growth is the fact that some people receive government services either free or for pennies on the dollar because of progressive taxation. Hopefully, the reader can also see that the "flat tax" is just another highly progressive tax that will intensify the disease that is laying waste to our country.

If we would tax everyone proportionately out of their own pocket with as close to a *uniform percentage* as possible on their consumption instead of their income, there would be little desire for most of our federal welfare bureaucracies and subsidies, because the great majority of the people who vote for such schemes would not want them once they had to pay for them proportionately with their own money. Thus, there would be little desire to retain the massive Leviathan in Washington that is running roughshod over our lives.

It is this issue of the need for genuine *rate uniformity* that must be grasped if sane and responsible government is ever to be restored in America. Yet the flat tax plans move us in the opposite direction — toward steeper progressivity. By trying to be popular with "the people" by granting large personal deductions, such proposals end up creating a huge underclass of citizens who receive government services for free, and thus they increase rather than decrease demand for government spending programs.

Flat Tax "Breaks" for the Rich

The third flaw in the flat tax proposals lies in their exclusions of certain capital income. It is not just the fact that low income earners avoid taxation under these plans that makes them so objectionable. Most of them give sops to the rich also by levying only wages and salaries while excluding earnings from capital investments. This creates an inequity because those who have substantial money in their lives and are in a position to live off their capital will pay *zero taxes* under this type of policy.

Flat tax plans, understandably, avoid taxing interest, dividends and capital gains in order to create incentive for economic growth; but it means the wealthy scions of leisure in Palm Beach end up paying *nothing* toward the maintenance of government while the working people of America have to pay 17 percent of their wages. This is just as unfair as the opposite feature of the flat tax: allowing four-member families to have a $33,300 deduction and thus escape taxation altogether. Under such a flat tax, both the upper and lower classes get substantial "breaks" with which to avoid paying their share. Who is left to hold the bag? Why, the productive middle class, of course. They have no lobbyists in Washington to petition the deal makers for special privileges.

Herein lies the major objection to the flat tax. Because of its highly skewed design, it dumps the lion's share of the tax burden squarely onto middle and upper class wage and salary earners. Most lower income earners will pay *nothing*, and many of the rich will pay *nothing*. This immense flaw dooms the flat tax to rejection by the American people, and deservedly so.

Flat taxers counter this reasoning with the claim that taxing savings and investment is taxing income "twice," which is unfair. This is only partly true. While taxing dividends is taxing income twice (at the corporate level and again at the individual level), it is not the case when dealing with interest earned on CD's and bonds and with capital gains income.

For instance, when a CD holder earns $1,000 in interest from a $20,000 deposit, he is receiving income that has never been taxed before. For some reason, however, conventional wisdom sees it differently.

As columnist Stephen Chapman puts it in a recent article, "When you earn income, it is taxed once. If you save it instead of spending it, you are then taxed a second time — on the interest it earns." Most economists, he intimates, view this as unfair. [29]

But is it? The $1,000 in interest is totally *new* income that the depositor is receiving for the first time and on which he has never been taxed. To tax this sum is not taxing income *twice*; it's taxing *additional* income that has been made from previous income. If we were taxing the $20,000 principal, then we would be taxing income "twice." But only the interest (the new income) is being taxed.

Flat taxers are engaging in a very tortured form of "logic" in an attempt to establish that taxation of interest is a *double* tax and therefore unfair. Take, for example, a recent article by former Delaware governor Pete du Pont in *Human Events*.

Mr. du Pont points out that if we earn $100 and pay 15 percent taxes on it, we are then free to spend the other $85. Under our system of taxation, we owe no more taxes. But if we save the $85 in the bank, the government is going to tax the interest we earn at the end of the year. This is unfair, he claims, because the interest earned is nothing but compensation for our relinquishing the use of our principal, and therefore not income.

"[T]hat interest," he declares, "is really compensation for something we have given up: the immediate use of our $85 and the immediate satisfaction we would have enjoyed by spending it. It is like an insurance payment we receive after a fire or a car accident: compensation for something we have lost. The interest does not add to our assets as much as it makes us whole after a loss." [30]

Yes, the interest is compensation for having given up the immediate use of the $85 and the enjoyment we would have received from spending it. But a wage earner has the same dilemma with the eight hours of energy he gives up to the factory for a day. He could have spent those eight hours by going fishing and received considerable enjoyment from them. But that doesn't mean his income from the factory is somehow not income because it is "compensation for something lost." All income, whether from the investment of energy or currency, is compensation for something lost.

Du Pont claims that, "interest does not add to our assets as much as it makes us whole after a loss." But the $85 principal is still intact and can still be spent, so there is no loss of capital. There is a delay of satisfaction from spending, but we are compensated for that delay. Likewise, the factory worker delays his satisfaction from fishing when he invests his eight hours in the factory, for which he is compensated.

Since both currency investor and energy investor are *compensated* for their delays, they should both be taxed on the compensation if we are going to employ an *income* tax. Income is income, whether it comes from currency or energy.

This same reasoning also applies to capital gains income. It is *new* income and should be taxed if we are employing an income tax system. However, among conservatives and libertarians, this view of capital gains taxation is not the predominant view. The more popular view has been expressed by the economist and supply-side guru, Jude Wanniski: "Capital gains should not be treated as income at all, in that they constitute a reward to the individual who risks aftertax ordinary income on the enterprise of another." [31]

The wage earner sees this as pure and simple favoritism. He could say the same thing about his earnings: "Overtime wages should not be treated as income at all in that they constitute a reward to the individual who risks after hours energy on the enterprise of his employer."

Capital gains are *new* profits that have not been taxed. Just because the income that was invested to earn those profits has already been taxed, this does not negate the fact that new income has been created.

Corporations take their profits that are taxed from one year and plow them back into expanding their business for the next year. Yet we don't hear anyone claiming that their second year profits from the purchase and sale of inventory should not be taxed because they stem from investment of their previous year's income that has already been taxed. Those second year profits are *new* income and therefore taxable. Capital gains from the purchase and sale of a stock are no different.

All income — profits, gains, salaries and wages, whether from capital or labor — requires "risk" of some kind and the "loss" of other options. The determining factor as to whether such income should be taxed is not the level of risk that is required, nor the loss of other options that is incurred, nor whether its origin is capital or labor, but whether or not it is *new* income. If it is new income previously untaxed, then it should be levied under an "income" tax system. But it should only be levied *once*. This is simple common logic, and it comports with the laws of equity.

Corporate dividends, however, are not equatable to interest and capital gains. A corporation stockholder is an owner of the issuing corporation that makes a product and reaps a profit. Once the corporation pays its 35 percent tax on its profits, dividends are then paid out of what is left. The stockholder should not have to pay an *additional* tax on those profits (which he does when his dividends are taxed again as individual income).

The Republican concept of flat taxation is an attempt to be truly growth stimulating. Therefore, it excludes taxation on interest and capital gains as well as dividend income. But since this opens up an unseemly loophole for the rich to pay *zero taxes* by simply living off their CD's, bonds and stock sales, such a plan loses its moral legitimacy.

In a recent *Wall Street Journal* article, the Nobel laureate in economics, James M. Buchanan, wrote in regards to this issue, "A uniform-rate tax on all income, by whomever received and in whatever form, with no exemptions or deductions, should be the primary revenue source in a society that values the *rule of law*. Such a flat tax eliminates... groups who lobby politicians for tax favors, and reduces gross conflicts of interest by requiring all persons to *pay some tax*.

"Confusion arises because the Dick Armey-Steve Forbes versions of a flat tax exempt savings and capital gains and allow generous deductions at low income levels, thereby removing both the normatively desirable feature of generality and reintroducing incentives for economic and political inefficiency." [32]

There is no way around this flaw for flat tax proponents except to apply their 17 percent rate to savings and capital gains income as well as to salaried income. This they don't wish to do, however, because it negates the main purpose of the flat tax by suppressing incentives for economic growth.

The solution to this dilemma is all too obvious: Tax *consumption* rather than *income*! Everyone consumes, and thus everyone will have to pay something toward the support of government. Since the rich consume far larger amounts than the poor, they will pay far larger amounts of taxes. But those "larger amounts" will be more proportional and thus fairer because of the more uniform rate. The denizens of places like Palm Beach and Martha's Vineyard consume billions in goods and services every year as they live off of their capital investments. The drug lords, black marketers and tax dropouts of the underground economy consume billions in goods and services every year also. Both of these massive sources of revenue would be reached with a national sales tax but left untouched by a flat tax on wage income.

Thus, by uniformly taxing consumption instead of income, we solve the two major problems of all tax systems — 1) how to assure that everyone pays a fair share toward the support of government, and 2) how to assure adequate incentive so as to produce vibrant economic growth.

Everyone, I think, will agree that there are no ideal tax systems; they all have flaws. But taxing *consumption* would be as close to the ideal as we could come, both practically and ethically. The flat tax, in order to be growth enhancing, must relinquish the moral high ground by conveying favors to the rich. A national sales tax does not have that problem. Since the political left will almost certainly marshal enough support to foil any income tax attempting to be growth enhancing by excluding capital income, why waste time with the flat tax? America desperately needs *growth enhancing* tax reform. Only a national sales tax can provide it and still tax everybody proportionately.

We can twist and manipulate statistics forever, defining income this way and then that way, and shifting the burden to this group and then that group. But after eight decades of reprehensible congressional finagling of the country's tax laws, all Americans who have brains to think should surely grasp by now that there can never be *fairness* in any kind of income tax system. Even if proportional rates could ever be achieved, the very nature of the income-profits engine that we propose to feed from is such that we destroy incentive, growth and prosperity with our efforts. The Founding Fathers were very wise to inhibit the Federal Government's power to tax our incomes. We must find our way back to that wisdom.

A national sales tax as outlined here, with its closeness to uniformity and with a two-thirds congressional majority required to raise it, is the fairest and most efficient means to tax free people. If the Federal Government was reduced to its legitimate constitutional functions, the entire structure could ultimately be financed with a sales tax as low as 7 percent. In this way, a man consuming $10,000 a year would pay *$700 in taxes*, a man consuming $100,000 a year would pay *$7,000 in taxes*, and a man consuming $1,000,000 a year would pay *$70,000 in taxes*. Thus, the richer and more productive members of society would pay more for the maintenance of government than the poorer and less productive (which is fair because they have more property and assets to be protected), yet they would not be penalized for their superior productiveness as they now are with the progressive income tax.

It is the men and women in the $25,000 to $75,000 income class that are being literally squeezed out of existence by our present tax system. It is the great middle class of America, the businessmen, merchants, professionals, specialists and skilled blue collar workers — in short, the *producers*. These are the ones paying for all the unconscionable waste of the government, all the grandiosity, all the senseless regulations, commissions and agencies that are stifling our economy and our freedom. It is these men and women who must stand up and protest vehemently if we are to stop the onslaught of Big Brother.

Close Cousins of the Income Tax

As we have just seen, taxes on capital income are certainly justified if we are going to employ an *income* tax. But all income (whether it derives from capital or labor) should only be taxed once, and it should not be redistributed. The point that this book is trying to make, however, is that we should not be taxing income *at all*. Therefore, not only the personal income tax but all other direct taxes on income and property need to be abolished. These are the corporation, capital gains, estate and gift taxes.

Mainstream political opinion in America has for years been antagonistic to "successful people" and the corporations, capital, and estates that they build in their lives. As a result, taxes in these three areas have become punitive and firmly entrenched (as if it is somehow evil to be intelligent, productive, energetic and daring — which are the qualities that go into forming businesses and building wealth). It is time to purge from our national ethos such an irrational vision of life.

Corporations, capital gains, and personal estates are not badges of iniquity to incur punishment from Big Brother. They are creations of productive prowess that arise from inspiration, perseverance and hard, honest toil. They are, by right, the possessions of those individuals who have brought them into being. When they are redistributed, then the men and women who made them are redistributed. This is certainly not what America is supposed to be about.

With the elimination of corporation taxes, an explosive increase in available funds for reinvestment into new expansion, technology and ideas would take place. Such an increase would create a boom in the economy the likes of which is inconceivable to the bureaucrat mentalities of modern day government. The profits of our business community are what create the investment funds needed for *new jobs and growth* for the people of this country (remember our lesson about "capital accumulation"). Without the right to keep such profits, companies cannot possibly be innovative and grow adequately — stagnation, recession, and ever higher levels of unemployment being the inevitable results. The same rationale also exists for capital gains taxes. Here lies one of the most onerous burdens placed upon America's economic growth by the liberal establishment.

Capital gains taxes are allegedly taxes on "evil plutocrats" who exploit the people by gouging obscene profits they don't deserve. Not so. Capital gains are the province of almost everyone in the middle class in any free-market society. Every industrious American who owns a home, some shares of stock, a mutual fund, a prosperous business, or buys and sells any object of escalating value, will eventually find himself subject to the capital gains tax.

The crime in all this is that Big Government has created a most unjust racket by combining progressive taxes on income with taxes on *non-existent* capital gains caused by inflation. Because today's dollars buy considerably less than those of yesterday, our "capital gains" often turn out not to be actual gains at all; yet, we are still raked for 28 percent by the Feds as if we increased our capital.

For example, John Gainswealth buys 1,000 shares of stock in Blue Chip Corporation in 1975 for $35 per share and sells them for $70 per share in 1995. The IRS then appears, hand outstretched, to demand 28 percent of the supposed $35,000 profit. It wants $9,800 from the sale price. But because inflation has created higher prices over the 20 years that Mr. Gainswealth held his stock in Blue Chip Corporation, he has actually lost in terms of real dollars on the investment. Since the Consumer Price Index has tripled from 1975 to 1995, his $70,000 in 1995 doesn't buy nearly as much as his $35,000 in 1975. So his "capital gain" is really a "capital loss." Yet he still has to pay 28 percent of the difference in purchase and sale prices.

What takes place here is thus a *triple theft* on the part of the Federal Government. Mr. Gainswealth has to first pay a highly progressive tax on his money as he earns it. Then through central bank induced inflation, he loses substantial purchasing power of his money saved, and in addition he has to pay a $9,800 tax on a "gain" that he never made. This is what goes by the name of *social justice* in the Alice in Wonderland world we inhabit today.

Such is the "reason and leadership" that guides contemporary tax policy. Continually pushing for higher and higher rates of taxation to feed its uncontrollable spending frenzies, an obtuse Washington actually *lowers* its revenue while decimating the lives and savings of American citizens. Oblivious to the laws of economics and human nature, Congress raised the capital gains tax in 1986 from 20 to 28 percent, claiming this would boost needed revenues. But investors aren't stupid. They merely decreased their capital gains transactions in order to avoid the increased tax. Thus, the base plummeted, and Washington now takes in less revenue with a 28 percent capital gains tax than was obtained with the old 20 percent rate.

But this is not the only damage. The 40 percent hike in capital gains taxes has thoroughly depressed venture-capital investments and frozen great amounts of personal capital holdings throughout the economy, whether in the form of real estate, businesses or stocks. This stultifies overall economic activity and growth, decreasing jobs and reducing wages for working people.

It is here in the creation of economic growth and jobs that the collectivist mindset wreaks so much of its damage on our country. Establishment liberals cry every election year that we need more growth and jobs, and that the Federal Government must spend more of our money on job bills, infrastructure renewal, inner city programs, etc. Yet all that is necessary to create jobs is to allow the American people to *retain their earnings,* much of which would become savings, which would then be readily invested into all sorts of new ventures and expansion of old ventures. Such ventures create jobs at the rate of 3 to 1 over equivalent "government investments" of those earnings. Moreover, they are *real jobs* with productive futures for individuals and the nation, not the *make-work jobs* that come from federal spending programs.

Jobs that are created from government investment of our earnings are mostly paper shuffling jobs that sustain indolent bureaucrats. This is because government officials don't have to make a profit, so they have no incentive to find and satisfy *real demand* in the market place. They can just "make work," and then preen on the nightly news telecasts as if they actually did something worthwhile.

On the other hand, what is created with private investment of our earnings are genuine economic growth jobs. This is because private investors (individuals, banks, corporations, mutual funds, insurance companies, etc.) seek to make a profit. Thus, they have a powerful incentive to put their money into promising businesses *for which there is a demand*, businesses that require real employees, that create genuine services and products that real people need to live and build their lives around.

If liberals and collectivists wish to create *real jobs* for America, they need only to get out of the way of the greatest job creation machine in the history of man—the American free-market economy. But such a machine needs private investment capital, which can only come from personal savings, which can only come from income, profits, or *capital gains.*

Cato Institute economist Stephen Moore has extensively analyzed the relation of capital gains taxation to economic prosperity in America over the past several decades. In a recent article, he reports that after the last two rate cuts (49 to 28 percent in 1978 and 28 to 20 percent in 1981), entrepreneurial investment and new business growth skyrocketed. Under the 49 percent rate in 1977, new venture-capital commitments in the U.S. registered *$70 million.* After the rate had been reduced to 20 percent, new venture-capital commitments soared to *$5.1 billion* in 1983, an astounding 700 percent increase. This was the beginning of the Reagan boom, which regrettably was marred by the dismal failure of Congress to reduce legislative spending and regulation accordingly, and then largely washed away by the Bush and Clinton administrations' return to conventional, high-tax, anti-growth policies. Nevertheless, a precise correlation is obvious to any open minded observer: prosperity and opportunity expand exponentially in the wake of strong capital gains rate cuts. [33]

When liberals advocate, with economically illiterate smirks on their faces, higher and higher capital gains taxes, they are tying massive anvils around the necks of all entrepreneurs in America (check out the weekly smirks of Al Hunt and Mark Shields on CNN's Capitol Gang). It is only entrepreneur personalities who create new business ventures for any nation. When the people's capital gains are confiscated by slothful bureaucracies, the entrepreneurial function atrophies and growth stagnates. It is no accident that the Pacific Rim economies of Southeast Asia are exploding in growth while we are stagnating. They have no capital gains taxes at all.

Slash capital gains and corporation taxes to zero, and a miraculous new America would spring forth — a robust, bustling, creative America possessed of hope-filled opportunities in every city and town for all industrious men and women.

The same also applies for estate and gift taxes. Because these are direct taxes on individuals which affect their incentive to produce, they act as just one more drag upon economic productiveness for the country. The socially injurious aspect of such taxes is that productive capital is destroyed in favor of *consumption*. Only a small proportion of the wealth of super-rich families is in the form of consumption items such as yachts, clothes, jewelry, automobiles, etc. The vast bulk of their wealth lies in *productive ventures*. Consequently, when government seizes 50 percent of the estate of a multimillionaire at time of death, it is seizing half of his productive assets that are employing workers and manufacturing goods and services. If said estate has a value of $50 million, then $25 million in capital (that could be used to produce more goods and services and thus higher wages and profits for all) has been removed from the marketplace to feed the ineptitude of Washington's bureaucracies, which consume such wealth by shoring up special interest factions.

Moreover, because estate taxes threaten the rich with confiscation of their wealth, the rich sometimes end up preferring to consume many of their assets during their lifetimes rather than relinquish them to the tax man at time of death. This shifts certain portions of their wealth from long-term productive ventures to short-term dissipation. All of society loses in proportion to the value of the productive ventures that are no longer maintained or are never created.

The most heinous aspect of estate and gift taxes, however, is that they violate our basic right to the property we have created. What moral right does any government have to prohibit men and women from passing on their businesses, their farms, their homes and their life's savings to their children, their friends, or their favorite charity? What is the sense of striving to produce in life if a man does not have the right to dispose of his own wealth *as he sees fit?* Wealth belongs to those who create it, not to "society."

Estate and gift taxes are the most blatant form of *double taxation* we can construct. An estate or a gift is the accumulation of wages, profits, interest and capital gains received throughout one's lifetime. All of these sources of income have already been taxed at the time they were earned. To tax them again at the time of death or upon giving them away is *outright theft.* What manner of man tells himself he is acting nobly while voting for the confiscation of another man's life's work?

Our present estate and gift taxes are not nobly designed for the good of human beings. Their purpose is to stop the accumulation of wealth by the *productive* people of this earth. Their intellectual roots lie in the socialist view that the accrual of large amounts of capital by one man or one family is somehow *unjust*. But what the statists — with their fawning supporting cast of guilt-ridden movie stars and aging New Left radicals — refuse to see is that all such accumulations of wealth are very beneficial to everyone. This is because such money is always *working somewhere* to create opportunities, jobs, ideas and prosperity — whether in the form of a bank account, a stock purchase, an insurance policy, or a private business. So long as such money is earned honestly there is no moral or practical justification for its expropriation when being willed or given to someone.

The man who applauds estate and gift taxation is, all too often, driven by envy of those better off than he and a subconscious desire to bring the productive and the affluent down to a lower level of life. Those who are wealthy and still support such confiscations are blindly obeying the prevailing orthodoxy of the collectivist intellectual establishment — afraid to contest its hackneyed, egalitarian moralizing for fear of appearing out of fashion with society's accepted authorities. Such envies and fears are not very lofty emotions to harbor.

Income Taxes Benefit Bureaucracy

The Washington establishment's excuse for huge confiscatory taxation (income, corporate, capital gains, estate, etc.) is not only that it is needed to run government, but also to further freedom and equal opportunity for the poor and ensure a productive economy. As the reader should now realize, this is the exact opposite of the truth. All that such taxation does is create *less freedom and opportunity*. It drives productive rebels underground, investment capital offshore, the rich into tax-exempt foundations to avoid the breakup of their estates, and everyone into *less productivity* because of the time, paper work, altered preferences, and demoralization resulting from such confiscation.

The ones who benefit from such seizures of wealth are not the poor. They're the millions upon millions of bureaucrats, civil servants, welfare counselors, professorial researchers and administrative drones who presently strut around the federal, state and local government hierarchies of this country, pontificating on the nation's "dire need" for more advisory commissions, regulatory bureaus, racial quota systems, busing agendas and sociological surveys as to why unwed mothers are so alienated from life. These are the beneficiaries of confiscatory taxation, not the poor — these nineteen million bureaucratic barnacles upon the ship's hull of our life's energy.

To verify this, we need only do some simple arithmetic. The amount of tax revenues that the Federal Government spent on cash and non-cash welfare benefits in 1995 came to $324 billion. According to official figures, there are 25 million people in America classified by the government as "poor." This means that there was approximately $13,000 available for every person below the poverty line in America ($324 billion divided by 25 million = $13,000). What happened? Why did they not receive it? If we had merely sent the money we collected out to the poor, the average person under the poverty level would have received an income of $13,000 for the year ($52,000 for a family of four). The War on Poverty would have been over. But this did not take place. Why? Because alleviation of poverty is not the goal of our federal welfare bureaucracies. If poverty was ended, their bureaucracies would no longer be needed, and thus their jobs would be ended.

William Simon, the former Secretary of the Treasury in the Ford administration, has estimated that approximately two-thirds of all social welfare expenditures *goes to the administrators,* and only one-third to the poor people themselves. [34] Out of that $324 billion that Washington confiscates from our paychecks, $216 billion is taken by the bureaucrats for salaries and administrative costs, and the remaining $108 billion is disbursed to the poor.

What this means is that the average person under the poverty level receives approximately $4,300 in support every year ($108 billion divided by 25 million = $4,300). The rest goes to pay for the millions of government officials and their army of social workers and professorial researchers, sitting behind their mahogany desks, running this vast empire. The average salary of a government employee in Washington, reported by *Industry Week,* is $48,200. The average salary of a taxpayer chump is $24,850.

What this tells us is that the entire federal welfare system should be phased out and replaced with local and private agencies. The poor people would then receive a far more legitimate level of support at far less cost to the American taxpayers. The hundreds of billions presently being allocated to government administrative costs would be unnecessary because the big welfare bill (going to the able-bodied) could be shifted to the private sector, and the small bill (going to the disabled) could be retained at the state government level. Privatizing welfare for able-bodied citizens would restructure its priorities from "permanent maintenance" to the "temporary helping hand" it was prior to the Great Society.

Charles Murray and Marvin Olasky have written the two definitive studies on this question of social welfare—*Losing Ground* in 1984, and *The Tragedy of American Compassion* in 1992.

These two renowned political theorists empirically demonstrate that massive federal welfare programs are not gallantly helpful to men and women, but in essence ignominiously harmful to them, and that the system of *private* welfare which was in place prior to the onset of 20th century statism was far more efficient, humane and just for all involved.

The bureaucratic welfare policies, championed by collectivist liberalism for the past 35 years, are inexcusably destructive to not only the overburdened taxpayers, but to the alleged beneficiaries — the poor people themselves — who have become entrapped in a degrading life of psychic squalor and despair.

The privatization solution to the welfare problem will become more and more obvious over the next decade as the Federal Government plunges deeper into debt and the American underclass sinks deeper into dependency. It is the only way to restore fiscal responsibility to the disbursements and motivation for escape to the recipients. Under such a reform, all government assistance programs for *disabled* men and women would be retained at the state government level, while all government assistant programs for *able-bodied* men and women would be phased into private agencies. The Federal Government would be phased out of the picture completely.

This would be both fiscally sound and morally proper. Able-bodied men and women would be thrust into the healthy discipline of the marketplace instead of being vitiated by the sloth of the Leviathan. Once the Federal Government is removed from the arena, private charities would mushroom to fill the void. Unlike government funded welfare, private charities are voluntary. Consequently, they will be much more selective of their recipients and much more adamant about said recipients striving to re-enter the work force as soon as possible. Government welfare bureaucracies instinctively seek to *increase* their caseloads so as to assure their continued existence as a bureaucracy. Private charities instinctively seek to *decrease* their caseloads because their motive is the spiritual goal of turning people's lives around. Thus, adequate relief for the needy would still be available as it was prior to 1960, but it wouldn't be the lavish, automatic subsidies without strings that the Great Society has given us.

America of the 21st century must come to grips with this momentous issue of welfare (and not just for the poor, but also for corporations, farmers, artists, etc.) We have heedlessly fashioned, over the past 50 years, a Great Handout Society for the *able-bodied*, a fantasy land of milk and honey entitlements where actions need no longer have consequences and where reality is not what it objectively is, but what we, with our tailored statistics and convenient sophistries, wish to believe it is. A day of reckoning is looming up ahead for Nanny State liberalism. We will either confront it with reason and self-reliance, or we will collapse into a bureaucratic wasteland of moroseness and bankruptcy.

If we return to the legacy our Founders bestowed upon us, then there is hope for the future. We can dismantle the federal Gargantua; we need only to reject the irrationality of socialism in all its disguises and accept the propriety of the free-market.

This is why the figure of a *7 percent* national sales tax is not unrealistic in the future. By phasing out (plank by plank) the great bulk of federal bureaucracies, with the few vitally necessary functions being retained through local, state and private agencies, there would be no necessity for a tax any higher than 7 percent. We don't need to be paying officious federal bureaucrats $216 billion every year to dispense $108 billion of our money to the poor. We, as Americans, can do *our own dispensing* locally and privately, and save much of the $216 billion that we now pay to Washington overlords.

Neither do we need to be paying $428 billion in FICA taxes every year. We could privatize Social Security and abolish all FICA taxes from worker paychecks and business earnings. Chile has already done so, and it has created a 26 percent savings rate in their economy. (See Peter J. Ferrara, "The New Politics of Social Security," *Wall Street Journal*, February 14, 1996, Jean A. Briggs, "A Political Miracle," *Forbes*, May 11, 1992, and Warren Brookes, "Chile Leads the Way on Social Security," *Boston Herald*, June 24, 1989.)

There are countless other innovative reductions that can also be made in the level of government we now have, which would save hundreds of billions of dollars. We don't have to endure this bloated monster in Washington. All that is necessary is for the American people to become aware of the truth of the situation and be motivated to take decisive action.

Many of us can remember a time when government wasn't such a bloated monster taking the lion's share of our earnings. It was during the far freer and more serene years after World War II between 1945-1960. Representative Chris Cox (R-Calif.) reflected back on that era in his testimony to the House Ways and Means Committee, June 7, 1995: "When I was a child in the 1950's, government did not consume 40 percent of our gross domestic product, but half that. As a result, the average American family, making the average national income, paid an income tax rate of just 2 percent. The average family of my parents' generation could afford a three-bedroom home, even though the norm was that only one spouse had to work. They paid only 4 percent interest on their 30-year mortgage. Their FICA tax rate was 1.5 percent. All of this was possible because — despite such extravagances as the Korean War, the G.I. Bill and the Marshall Plan — the federal budget was balanced in a low-tax environment.

"That kind of freedom and opportunity is again possible in our future. But it will become reality only if we are actually willing to reduce the size of government and only if we recognize that the income tax, in the American context, is an experiment that has been tried and has miserably failed."

A Need for Moral Courage

To sum all this up, there is one issue today that transcends in importance all others in the domestic political arena: the Federal Government's ability to *progressively tax the incomes* of the American people. The grotesque, overweening bloat of welfare statism depends upon Washington's utilization of this power.

By taxing people's incomes at punitive and progressive rates, the Federal Government can continue to finance ever-increasing statist programs and bureaucracies. And congressional legislators can continue to win election after election by promising to expropriate more and more wealth from the productive to hand out to the non-productive. The way to stop the runaway growth of the Federal Government is to end its capacity to employ this technique. A replacement of the income, corporate, capital gains, estate and gift taxes with a *national sales tax* requires nothing more than firm conviction and moral courage on the part of all those who work for a living in this country and are willing to fight for the right to keep what they create. We, the producers of America, must simply take an uncompromising stand. Big Government spenders have exploited our benevolence for far too many years now in order to feed their power lust and their guilt.

If men are to have meaning in life, both materially and spiritually, then they must be able to make their own choices as to where and how their own income is to be spent. Any other form of existence is empty servitude. Those who don't, or won't, realize this are the reasons why Washington has erected the dictatorial bureaucracies of welfarism that so omnipresently manipulate our lives today.

America was meant for the free, for the self-reliant, for those individuals who are willing to live on their own wits, energy and courage. She was never supposed to have a federal income tax. She was never supposed to have a powerful centralized maze of bureaucracies regimenting and subsidizing every aspect of our lives. America stood for *limited government* and *personal independence* at the outset, and unless she restores that stand, there will be no true liberty or justice for men on this earth in the future.

CHAPTER TWO

Questions and Answers About the National Sales Tax

For most Americans, the national sales tax is a new concept that they know very little about. As a result, there are numerous questions that come to mind as to why the NST is so necessary for America, how it would work, and what its consequences will be for our lives. What follows are some of the more common questions that are heard from people throughout the country, and answers to them.

Wouldn't a 16 percent national sales tax combined with most states' 7 percent sales taxes be awfully burdensome?

Keep always in mind that the national sales tax does not *add* 16 percent to our taxes; it *replaces* 15 to 39 percent taxes that we pay on income. It *replaces* 28 percent taxes that we pay on capital gains. It *replaces* 15 to 39 percent corporation taxes which are passed on as higher prices. It *replaces* all estate and gift taxes. This certainly negates any "burdensome" effect that might be felt. The real issue is, would we rather pay 16 percent of our consumption or 15 to 39 percent of our income and profits to the Federal Government?

Also remember that 16 percent is just the starting point in order to remain revenue neutral and not increase the deficit. As the economy dramatically expands in productivity because of the new tax system, the base will expand noticeably. This will allow the 16 percent rate to be brought down to the 10 to 12 percent range, and eventually even to the 7 to 8 percent range as we strip Washington of its bureaucratic power in the upcoming years.

Won't the national sales tax greatly aggravate the federal deficit problem?

The federal deficit has come about not because we tax too little but because we spend too much. As we saw earlier, the U.S. Treasury's revenues under a 16 percent NST will be *more* than they are under our present income tax system. Also, because of the boom in economic productivity that will take place upon enactment of the NST, a larger base from which to obtain revenues will result, which will create even a larger surplus over present revenues from the income tax.

Switching to an NST will therefore help the deficit problem. Of course, to *solve* the deficit problem rather than just *help* it, Congress is going to have to curb its profligate spending. This will require leadership and courage on its part, and a willingness from all Americans to ask less of their government and more of themselves.

The primary problem here is that federal expenditures are exploding because we as voters have demanded that Congress provide us with a continually growing cornucopia of "government benefits." This explosion of demand has come about because of *progressive taxation* and the promise of something for nothing, i.e., receiving benefits at the expense of those higher up on the earning ladder. Since not nearly enough tax dollars can be extracted from the rich and semi-rich to pay for all the demands, Congress resorts to running a chronic deficit to make up the difference, which it funds by massive borrowing from the earnings of future generations to gratify our demands of today and assure itself re-election. Thus, the two policies of progressive taxation and deficit spending feed on each other. An end to this insanity will never come about through the policy of raising taxes, but only by radically lowering our demands for government benefits. Raising taxes merely exacerbates the destructive spending spiral that we're caught up in because it puts *more* money into the hands of spendthrift legislators who then rush compulsively to promise *more* government benefits during election year in order to buy the allegiance of *more* voters. It's like pouring gasoline on a bonfire because politicians cannot stop themselves from employing the technique of buying votes with the promise of more benefits anymore than an alcoholic can stop himself from drinking. It's the nature of the political animal — grant him more revenues and he will always use those revenues to purchase larger constituencies rather than pay for previous promises. So a balanced budget will never be achieved with *higher taxes*. It will only be achieved when we as citizens radically reduce our demands for government benefits and radically reform our tax system. Anything short of this is illusory.

What are rebates? And should they be part of the NST?

Rebates are being proposed by some people in the sales tax movement so as to lessen the burden of the NST on the lower income earners and help assure its passage. They propose, for example, that the 16 percent tax on the first $4,000 of everyone's consumption be returned by the government. This would create a floor below which no one would be taxed.

If Congress sets the consumption level to be rebated at $4,000 for every adult and child, this would mean that a family of four would receive a rebate check from Washington every year for $2,560 ($16,000 x .16 = $2,560). A family of three would receive a rebate check of $1,920; a family of five, a rebate of $3,200, and so on.

The danger of such a policy is that the use of "rebates" with a consumption tax is like the use of "deductions" with an income tax. It gives the government the power to create a steeply progressive tax structure. Rebates can, if set high enough, lead to the same dilemma we face under Armey's flat tax which employs substantial deductions and creates a vast constituency of voters paying *zero taxes*.

Congress would have to establish the dollar amount of the rebates and would be under constant pressure to increase the amount every election year, thus buying the allegiance of more and more voters. It is conceivable that through manipulation of the rebates a huge FDR-like constituency could eventually be assembled in which 30 to 35 percent of the consuming public pays zero taxes. This constituency would be totally wedded to the welfare state and its perpetuation.

For example, if the rebates were to be raised by Congress from $4,000 to $6,000, then the average family of four would have $24,000 worth of consumption *tax free*. A family of five would have $30,000 worth of consumption *tax free*. And those families in the $40,000 and $50,000 consumption classes would pay *next to nothing* for government services. What incentive would these voters have to reduce government services that they are getting either free or for next to nothing? Congress wouldn't even have to raise the tax rate in order to pay for the increased rebates; it could enact rebate increases into law every few years as the tax base grows.

Thus, rebates could be used to further entrench the power of the bureaucratic state. Washington would be disbursing hundreds of billions of dollars with an accessible power to increase such disbursements. Can we trust Congress to responsibly administer such a power? It's very doubtful.

Sales tax advocates need to understand that the real generator of government growth for the past 80 years has been not just the income tax, but the *progressive* income tax. The arch enemy of freedom is progressivity. It does America no good to replace a highly progressive "income" tax with a highly progressive "consumption" tax. We won't have purged the real poison from the system. If Jefferson and the Founders were alive today, they would be heaping scorn upon all tax reform plans that avoid confronting the real issue: *highly progressive rates* whether in an income or consumption context.

In addition to their weakness on grounds of principle, rebates would also be highly inefficient. Why tax money away from people and then return it, when we could accomplish the same effect through exemptions? It is far better to leave the money in the people's pockets where it belongs.

Of course, a policy of exemptions is not exactly flawless either. They can be misused by Congress to favor certain voting factions in order to gain their support at election time (e.g., the food and housing industries, the medical field, transportation, etc.). It would appear, however, that there is less danger of abuse with exemptions than with rebates. Also, the use of exemptions does not create categories of voters who pay *zero taxes*.

As we saw earlier, all that is needed to lighten the burden of the NST on low income earners is to exempt the mainstays of food and housing from taxation, which creates a structure in which they pay less than they presently do under the income tax. Such a policy sufficiently balances the tax bite among all classes and brings us close to a uniform rate. Most importantly, it requires all citizens to contribute *something* toward the maintenance of government because everybody consumes non-exempt items such as gasoline, clothing, entertainment, etc. Only in this manner can we truly establish a responsible Congress.

Lightening the load of taxes on low income earners is something that we should surely try to achieve. But we should pursue it through lessening the control and power that government has in all our lives, rather than by creating "special breaks" in the tax laws for specific classes of people. We should decrease the amount of government spending for everyone, and the burden of government would then be lightened for the lower income earners. This is the only healthy and just means to accomplish such a goal.

Why are only food and housing exempted?

Only so many industries can be exempted without lowering the tax base drastically. If the base is lowered too much, it will require a very high rate, which eventually becomes unacceptable to the public.

By exempting food and housing, a rate structure that is fair for the lower income earners is established. It is a rate structure that is probably as close to uniformity as we can hope for at this juncture in history. Any further exemptions would just create more progressivity, which would destroy the primary purpose of tax reform — which is the need to move away from progressivity.

Food and housing are the two mainstay items in human lives, so they are the logical candidates to be exempted. Since the line has to be drawn somewhere, it makes sense to do so by limiting it to those items that are people's primary consideration in life, i.e., food and a roof over their heads.

Why should we exempt anything? Why not pass an NST that has no "exemptions" and no "rebates" period?

This is a policy that we should eventually implement. If there were to be no exemptions and no rebates, then the *base* would be considerably higher which would allow the *rate* to be set much lower — at 12 percent instead of 16 percent.

The problem with initiating this option immediately is that it would necessitate substantially raising the "effective" tax rates of all low income earners. For example, under our present progressive system, an individual making $13,000 annually pays an effective rate of about 8 percent after his standard deduction of $6,400. If we enacted a 12 percent sales tax with no exemptions or rebates, his taxes would go from 8 percent of "income" to 12 percent of "consumption." This would not only be unfair, but unpassable in Congress.

Since all taxpayers presently enjoy a standard deduction under our income tax system, any switch to a consumption tax system should provide some form of similar deduction (i.e., exemption) to prevent those in the lower income levels from having their taxes raised. This is simple logic in both a practical and a moral sense. As soon as possible, however, all exemptions should be eliminated. This could take place when the Federal Government's expenditures are sufficiently reduced to require approximately an 8 to 10 percent rate for its funding. Eliminating the exemptions would then allow us to further drop the rate to around 6 percent. At these low levels, the difference between rates with exemptions and rates without is slight enough that such a plan perhaps could be passed by Congress. This would then be the ultimate in simplicity and legitimacy, for Congress would have *no tax favors to convey* to any specific groups of voters, and the "uniformity principle" of the Constitution would be restored.

If we are supposed to be equal in America, shouldn't we encourage a progressive tax that equalizes earnings?

We are not supposed to be equal in America in any way except before the law. We all have equal "rights" in this country, but we are not and were never meant to have equal "results" created for us by a regimental government. Any government philosophy that sets out to equalize the earnings of its citizens will by necessity usurp their rights in the process.

There will always be a natural disparity in status, wealth and life-styles among free people, because there is a natural disparity in human abilities and ambitions. To try to level such disparities with government redistribution schemes (such as progressive taxation) is contrary to everything this country has stood for over two centuries. The Founders knew well that there can never be justice with such a tax philosophy. This is why the income tax must be repealed and replaced with a national sales tax.

Isn't the national sales tax merely a windfall for the rich?

Certainly not. It will benefit all income levels because it will create an explosion in investment capital and economic growth, thus raising real wages for the poor as well as profit levels for the affluent.

Noted economist Dr. John H. Qualls, in testimony submitted to Congress, reported that the formal studies he conducted demonstrated that higher standards of living would quickly result from the NST, and that the average take home pay for the American family would increase by more than $3,000 annually. [35]

Naturally, some will benefit more than others because they work harder, but all Americans (both rich and poor) will have their living standards raised by the NST.

If the NST is such a good idea, why are so many politicians and pundits against it?

Great ideas are almost always opposed by men in power when those ideas threaten the power that those men have accrued. The NST radically threatens the power structures of America because it will allow the people *who produce wealth* to retain it. It will eliminate many of the special interests that dominate Washington and feed off confiscatory taxation. This is not an enjoyable scenario to contemplate if you are tied into those special interests and the bureaucratic machinations they partake in.

The writers, scholars and politicians who are condemning the national sales tax are guided by the ideology of "mass bureaucratization." They cannot conceive of America without amassment of power in Washington. Not only are their financial livelihoods at stake here, but their intellectual and emotional commitments over many years are being challenged. Their response to the NST is a normal human reaction when one's lifestyle and guiding ideology are called into question.

There seems to be a basic law of human nature that compels almost all entrenched authorities to oppose radical change even when that change will bring about a demonstrably better society. This law springs from the fact that once an individual has lived his life past age 40 based upon certain fundamental philosophical premises, it is next to impossible for him to change those premises — even when they are shown to be fatally flawed.

Scientists, who have spent years of their lives in support of a certain paradigm, will forsake all the pledges of objectivity that comprise their creed to vehemently fight against a new paradigm that clearly presents a more rational perspective. Truth, the most highly prized goal of all, is forsaken to protect personal reputations and previous convictions.

Sadly, the same is true of almost all humans in every area of endeavor. Once an individual has committed a great number of years of his life working for certain political goals and the ideological premises that support those goals, he will fight tooth and nail to defend those goals and premises even as the country descends into hellacious ruin because of them.

This was the predicament of the Communists in the Soviet Union throughout the last two decades of their reign from 1969 to 1989. History's verdict was in. State socialism was a morbid, tyrannical and unworkable philosophy of social organization. It stifled all the requisites of prosperity and freedom. It decimated the human spirit. It was living death. Yet the intellectual and political authorities of the communist bloc shut their eyes to these unwelcome facts of reality and marched imperviously on for two more decades, shoring up their sham with lies, sophistries and doctored statistics.

The statist intellectual and political authorities of the West operate under this same law of human nature. Once past 40 years of age, it is well nigh impossible for them to admit they have committed themselves to a false political ideology that promotes irrational policies. Those pundits and politicians who have championed the massive interventionist state (sustained by progressive taxation) throughout the sixties, seventies and eighties are not going to readily endorse limited government and radical tax reform in the nineties. It would require having to admit that they have lived their entire lives on a fallacy. Unless such authorities are possessed of unusually strong character and clarity of vision, they will not be able to admit to such. They will, instead, proceed to do what the Communists did. They will slam the windows of their minds shut and continue to fight for their welfare state vision of governing and taxing, despite its rampantly destructive results.

This is why there is opposition from Washington and the media to the NST. To a large degree, defenders of income taxation are caught up in this syndrome of "defending their life's philosophical commitment" in face of its rapidly collapsing justification. The pundits and politicians who are denouncing the national sales tax are merely circling their ideological wagons in order to hopefully save their statist governing philosophy.

Can we have Congress pass the national sales tax into law right away, or do we need to pass an amendment to the Constitution first in order to assure that the income tax is abolished for good?

We need to do both. Passage of a constitutional amendment is mandatory. We, as a people, can never rest until the Sixteenth Amendment is repealed. Only in this way can we be absolutely certain that Congress will not reinstate the income tax in the future when the political climate has changed.

But as Stephen Moore of Cato Institute has pointed out, we can work on these two goals (passage of the NST into law and repeal of the Sixteenth Amendment) separately and simultaneously. We need not wait until the states have ratified an amendment abolishing the income tax for good before we enact the national sales tax into law. Congress can pass the NST tomorrow, while we proceed with generating the necessary support for repeal of the Sixteenth and the income tax. Our protection lies in combining with the NST a provision requiring a "two-thirds vote" of Congress in order to raise any federal tax (including the income tax which will be reduced to zero).

The times we live in require radical reform. America needs the national sales tax now, not 10 years from now. And it might well take 10 years to get the necessary amendment to repeal the Sixteenth ratified through the states.

Yes, Europe has ended up with both an income and a sales tax, but Europe does not have the "two-thirds vote" provision as protection. Besides, America is not Europe; Americans have a much stronger tradition of freedom and anti-tax sentiment than Europeans. It is unlikely that the American people would allow their congressmen to saddle them with *both* a sales tax and an income tax in these anti-Washington times.

Moreover, once the IRS apparatus and the income tax structure are dismantled, it would be very difficult to reconstruct them with a *two-thirds super majority* in Congress required to increase taxes. This gives us a strong protection against re-enactment of the income tax. Repeal of the Sixteenth will give us even stronger protection.

What about charitable deductions? Won't relief for the poor be lowered considerably without the incentive of these write-offs?

This view of human charity is incredibly cynical. The charitable institutions of America certainly thrived prior to the Sixteenth Amendment and the federal income tax, and they will thrive afterwards. We live in a turbulent and truculent era awash in confusion over many values, but there is one certainty the American people are clear on — the imperative to lend a helping hand to those who are struggling.

Out of the billions that are donated every year in this country to churches, hospitals and eleemosynary organizations, the overwhelming majority of such money comes from the hearts of prospective givers. This will not change under a national sales tax. On the contrary, because everyone will earn more money in an economy devoid of the income tax burden, there will be a *rise* in charitable donations. Charitable contributions rose dramatically under Reagan when he lowered the tax rate from 70 percent to 28 percent. The more people make, the more they give. The new tax system and the booming prosperity it ushers in will spur the natural inclinations of all men to help their fellows who are in need.

Won't real estate sales suffer without the mortgage-interest deduction, and won't many home owners have to sell their houses without it?

Under all national sales tax plans being considered, interest on loans is *not* taxed. Therefore, the interest component on one's mortgage is exempt as it is under our present income tax system. Only the price of the house (i.e., the principal loan amount) will be taxed.

This will increase the price of housing initially and perhaps create a temporary slackening in the industry, but any slow down will be followed quickly by a strong pick-up as long-term interest rates plunge due to the increase in savings and capital formation brought on by the economy's release from the monumental disincentives of the income tax system. Lower interest rates will *decrease* home payments which will *spark demand* for homes. This combination of lower interest rates and a more rapidly growing economy will ignite the housing industry as it will all other industries.

Many economists estimate that the huge increase in the savings pool brought on by the switch to a national sales tax will result in a 25 percent drop in long-term interest rates. A homeowner with a $100,000 mortgage at 8 percent would then have to pay only 6 percent. This would compute out to about $137 monthly savings on his payment, or a yearly savings of $1,644.

Under the national sales tax, a married homeowner (making $30,000 annually) will have both lower mortgage payments and lower taxes. His "effective" tax rate is reduced from about 10.5 percent of income ($3,169) to 9 percent of consumption ($2,720). He comes out ahead both ways.

In the long run, the real estate industry will benefit immensely from the national sales tax. Any price increase of homes will be more than balanced by decreases elsewhere.

Wouldn't a national sales tax have an inflationary effect upon the economy by raising the prices of all goods and services?

Not really. Price inflation is caused by monetary inflation on the part of the Federal Reserve, not by the enacting of taxes. It comes about when the Fed expands the quantity of money in circulation at a faster rate than goods and services are being produced in the economy.

While the NST does raise the prices of all goods and services initially, it will have a stimulatory effect upon savings and investment, which will greatly increase production of goods and services, i.e., their supply. This will create a lowering of general prices in the long run (assuming the Fed does not increase the money supply at too fast a pace).

Also, corporations will no longer have to pay income taxes which are factored into the costs of their products and services. So there will be a lowering of prices as the new lower cost structures of all businesses work their way through the competitive marketplace. This will balance out any initial bump in prices brought on by the national sales tax.

Establishment statists and many of those on Wall Street argue the contrary here. In their view, the "increased growth" generated by the NST would heat up the inflationary fires by fueling wage pressure and consumer demand. Because of this, they claim, we must accept a "slow growth" economy and be satisfied with a 2 to 2.5 percent annual expansion of the GDP. The old growth rules have changed. We must now resign ourselves to lower expectations.

The flaw in such reasoning is the assumption that high economic growth must *automatically* be accompanied by price inflation, a correlation which is not mandatory at all. If economic growth is brought about by "monetary expansion" on the part of the Fed, it is indeed inflationary; but if economic growth comes from "increased productivity" on the part of businesses and labor, it is *not* inflationary.

The Washington establishment is still imprisoned in the Keynesian fallacy of economic growth requiring expansive monetary policy through the Federal Reserve. Liberals and Big Government conservatives have never been able to grasp the fact that since a low tax policy leaves more money in private pockets, it increases incentive, innovation, efficiency and productivity, and brings increased economic growth *without price inflation*. This is because a low tax policy does not expand the money supply, but merely transfers existing capital from inefficient users to efficient users — i.e., from bureaucrats who consume it to entrepreneurs who invest it.

The proof of this can be found in the statistical records of our economic history over the past 150 years. The most telling example, as we have already seen, is the period of strong economic growth from 1870 to 1913 (4.3 percent annually) accompanied by an actual *deflation* of prices. The deflation of prices resulted from the fact that there was no excessive monetary expansion because there was no Federal Reserve during this period of our history.

When economic growth is created by leaving capital in entrepreneurial hands, i.e., by lowering taxes, it is *not* inflationary. It is only when the Federal Government tries to force economic growth through expansive monetary policy on the part of the Federal Reserve that it becomes inflationary. Both Washington and Wall

Street must come to accept this vital truth if we are to create an optimistic, prosperous and just society in America for the 21st century. It is easy to understand why the Washington establishment does not want to face this fact of economic reality. It would mean that its fiscal philosophy is (and has been for 60 years) theoretically wrong. Accepting such a truth would mean relinquishing substantial power to the private sector, which government establishments naturally hate to do.

What is perplexing is why Wall Street continues to cling to this fallacy of high economic growth automatically being inflationary. The policy behind the growth determines whether it will be inflationary or not. Is such growth brought about by Fed monetary expansion, or is it brought about by leaving more capital in entrepreneurial hands by means of lower taxes? There is a lot of difference in the two policies.

What about the claim that we don't need to radically alter our tax system at all, that instead we should just concentrate on reducing taxes through reduced government spending?

Surprisingly, there are numerous conservatives and libertarians who espouse this line. They want lower tax rates brought about by lower government spending but have resigned themselves to the income tax system with all its special breaks and loopholes. They feel that switching to a consumption based tax system is implausible and risky. Leave the tax system alone, they maintain, and concentrate instead on tax relief through substantial spending reductions.

The problem with this type of thinking is that substantial spending reductions will never be achieved *within a progressive tax system.* This is because tax "progressivity" and its "special breaks" conveyed to select groups are what create unconstrained government spending. As we have seen, when large groups of voters (from both lower and upper classes) are allowed the privilege of paying nothing and next to nothing in taxes, an irresponsible electorate evolves that demands steady expansion of government services and subsidies. This is basic human nature. If government benefits are free (or nearly free), demand for them will be infinite.

Overcoming this infinite demand for spending will be impossible until we radically reform the system, i.e., until all "special breaks" and the policy of "progressivity" are abolished. This will necessitate the adoption of a uniform tax system.

It will also necessitate switching from an income based to a consumption based system, so as to increase economic productivity and create a faster-growing revenue base. This will allow us to achieve far greater prosperity and far lower tax rates than we could ever achieve under an income tax system.

We can genuinely reduce government under a "consumption" tax that is *uniform*, but we will be plagued forever with expanding government under an "income" tax that is *progressive*. Therefore, it makes no sense to leave our tax system alone and attempt to reduce taxes merely by reducing government spending. Reduced government spending cannot be realized in any substantive way until the system itself is radically altered.

What about FICA taxes? What will happen to them?

Under the 16 percent NST, they will remain as they are. There are some in the sales tax movement who advocate elimination of these payroll taxes also. Daniel J. Pilla is one such advocate, and he has written a masterful book, *How To Fire The IRS*, that outlines his plan. If food and housing are excluded from taxation, we would need a sales tax in the range of 26 percent to accomplish such a plan, however, which would appear to be a hard sell to the American people. Far better to leave FICA taxes alone for the present and concentrate on the income, corporate, capital gains, estate and gift taxes.

There are other ways to eliminate FICA taxes. For example, if the public can be made aware of how much property and land is held by the Federal Government without constitutional authority, we could bring about a congressional sell off of these properties. A great portion of Social Security's $5 trillion liabilities (and maybe even all) could be paid with the proceeds. Libertarian Party presidential candidate, Harry Browne, has suggested that the Federal Government use these proceeds to purchase private annuities for all Social Security recipients and thus eliminate the government's involvement in the program. With such a privatization plan, we would no longer need FICA tax revenues, and these payroll taxes could be totally eliminated.

It is important to emphasize here that any privatization of Social Security should go further than the method adopted by Chile in the 1980's (which is the model being advocated in most privatization proposals). Chile's program is still *mandatory* as to participation and as to the amount of one's contribution. A true American privatization program should not only allow Social Security payments to be put into private annuities, but it should also be *totally voluntary* as to how much each American wishes to devote to such an annuity. We, as individual American citizens, should decide exactly what level of contribution we wish to save for our retirement — not the bureaucrats in Washington.

What would happen to the tax advice industry and the IRS? Wouldn't they all be out of work?

Most of them will be, but this should not be considered as detrimental. They will merely have to find employment where there is demand for their services. This is the price we pay to live in a free country. The rest of us live under such a possibility all the time in our industries. Why not IRS agents and tax advisers?

America was originally meant to be a nation of freedom in which no group of citizens can use government to feed off the efforts and earnings of other citizens. With the passage of the federal income tax in 1913, and the explosive growth of taxes through implementation of the New Deal and the Great Society, this original ideal has been destroyed.

By abolishing the federal income tax (along with all the other direct taxes on profits and savings), we will abolish the IRS from our lives, and thus the 115,000 agents who are feeding off our efforts and earnings. In addition, the great bulk of citizens who live off the "redistribution game" inherent in the welfare state philosophy will have to rethink their lives' direction and purpose. This can only result in a stronger, healthier and freer country. Rather than a detriment, this is a goal of inestimable benefit that all Americans should strive enthusiastically to achieve.

How long would it take to lower the NST to the 10 percent range?

This would depend on how much we cut government expenditures. If entitlement spending is held in check and certain major bureaucracies are terminated, the 16 percent rate could be lowered to the 10 percent range *within 10 years* because of the increase in the base due to our switch to consumption taxation.

For example, according to the U.S. Department of Commerce, the nation's consumption expenditure base grew at an average of 6.5 percent annually from 1987 to 1993 (with the low year being 4.0 percent in 1990 and the high year being 9.5 percent in 1987). Let's assume that by switching from income to consumption taxation our 6.5 percent average growth rate can be increased to 8.5 percent. The nation's consumption expenditure base (with groceries and housing exempted) was $4,051 billion in 1993 and would have produced $648 billion in sales tax revenues at a 16 percent rate. Using this base figure as our starting point, we would then have a $9,152 billion base in 10 years which would produce $915 billion in revenues at a 10 percent rate.

If during this 10 year period we would ax major bureaucracies such as HUD, Commerce, Energy, Education, etc., limit entitlement spending to a 3 percent increase annually, and turn off the spigot of special interest subsidies to corporations, farmers, artists, etc., we would have a leaner Federal Government that could easily be run on $915 billion in sales taxes.

If this were to take place, the average working man in America making $25,000 annually, who presently pays $2,966 in income taxes, would pay only $1,700 in sales taxes on consumption of $17,000 ($8,000 in food and housing being exempted). This is a *43 percent reduction.* Those on the low end of the scale making $13,000 annually, who presently pay $994 in income taxes, would pay only $600 in sales taxes on consumption of $6,000 ($7,000 being exempted). This is a *40 percent reduction.* Moreover, these taxpayers would have no IRS to contend with, and because of the resulting economic boom, they would be making more money than they were 10 years earlier.

If we would also require the Federal Government to liquidate all of its excess lands and properties and pay off Social Security liabilities during this 10-year period, then every worker's 7.65 percent FICA taxes could be eliminated. The Federal Government's hold over the American workingman's paycheck would be broken.

In addition, because all businesses would no longer have to contribute 7.65 percent to their employees' Social Security payments, wages would rise accordingly. It is commonly accepted by most economists that the 7.65 percent employer taxes that go into Social Security result in lower wages for their employees. By eliminating this burden on employers, a large portion of their subsequent savings would be channeled (due to market competition) into *higher wages* for employees.

All Americans could then invest whatever they choose into private annuities for their retirement, which would pay them many times more in return for far less dollars invested than the coercive and corrupt Social Security program now doles out to them. This would also allow the nation to keep an additional $400 billion per year in the private sector (the Federal Government siphoned off $428 billion in Social Security taxes in 1993). This would expand savings and lower interest rates dramatically, further stoking the furnace of economic growth.

Life in America with no income taxes would be a giant step toward that "shining city on a hill" that Ronald Reagan so eloquently urged us to pursue. Can it happen? It can if the people of America will not let themselves be bamboozled by liberal demagoguery, and if they will return to the philosophical vision of their Founders. If the American people will resolve to take back their freedom and its concomitant responsibility of self-reliance, if they will resolve to stand up to an arrogant and myopic federal establishment that clearly cares more for regimentation than rights, then that shining city can indeed be brought about.

CHAPTER THREE

Sales vs. Flat: The Great Debate

In July of 1995, *Reason* magazine published a symposium on the merits of the national sales tax versus the flat tax. Edward H. Crane of Cato Institute and Daniel J. Pilla presented the case for a *sales* tax. Bruce Bartlett, a senior fellow with the National Center for Policy Analysis, and Grover Norquist, the president of Americans for Tax Reform, presented arguments in favor of the *flat* tax.

Mr. Bartlett and Mr. Norquist each made a half-dozen or so objections to the national sales tax in the article, attempting mightily to paint the NST in a disparaging light. Mr. Bartlett also wrote a similar attack on the NST in the July/August 1995 issue of *American Enterprise.* Seeing that their objections parallel those of many in the flat tax movement, it is vital to understand the flaws in their reasoning, how they are misperceiving the NST, and in several instances grossly misrepresenting it. These learned men are overlooking one immensely important point when they claim that the "administrative difficulties" of the national sales tax will be insurmountable. And thus, they are using invalid comparisons to try and demonstrate its inefficacy.

Let's investigate their concerns and see if America should follow their prescriptions, or if she should harken back to her Founders, those sages of Philadelphia who saw in all taxes on income the gravest of dangers to the liberty and prosperity of independent men.

I have listed below the Bartlett objections from *Reason*, followed by answers for each, and likewise for Mr. Norquist. I have also answered, where appropriate, objections Mr. Bartlett made in *American Enterprise*.

THE BARTLETT OBJECTIONS

Objection #1 — The national sales tax would require too high a rate, approximately 32 percent.

If FICA taxes are left alone for the time being, a 16 percent rate will be more than enough to eliminate our income, corporation, capital gains, estate and gift taxes, which totaled $639 billion in 1993. Total expenditures on domestic and imported goods and services in 1993 were $5,102 billion according to the U.S. Department of Commerce as reported in *The World Almanac* 1995. This figure, however, does not represent what the probable tax base will be. To compute the probable base, we need to factor in the increased growth due to our switch from income to consumption based taxation. We then need to subtract expenditures on items such as food (consumed off premise) and housing. This is assuming that Congress excludes these categories rather than uses rebates so as to make the NST less burdensome to lower income groups.

For example, everyone (except hardcore leftists still operating under the delusions of Marxian economics) acknowledges that an NST would spur a considerable increase in economic growth because savings will no longer be taxed. This will naturally increase the tax base. Exactly how much is impossible to say, but a $200 billion increase would certainly not be inconceivable. This is in line with John H. Quall's Washington University econometric study done for C.A.T.S. This figure, when added to the $5,102 billion base, creates a total base of $5,302 billion. If Congress exempts grocery and housing expenditures ($1,051 billion in 1993), the taxable base would be $4,251 billion. Sixteen percent of this would be *$680 billion,* clearly in excess of the necessary $639 billion. (The effect of evasion on these figures will be discussed shortly.) As to what to do about FICA taxes at the 16 percent rate, they would remain the same until a privatization plan for Social Security is enacted. Until that time, their collection could be handled in one of two ways: 1) the Social Security Administration could collect them itself, or 2) the state governments could be required to collect them and turn them over to the Social Security Administration, and be compensated accordingly. The latter is the better method. Since businesses already collect FICA taxes from all employees, they could simply dispatch these revenues along with their sales tax revenues to the state governments to be forwarded to Washington. In this way, all IRS dealings with both individuals and businesses would be terminated, and the agency *would be totally abolished.* The Federal Government would then be required to collect both its sales tax revenues and its FICA taxes from the state governments only.

Would the state governments be willing to collect FICA taxes and turn the funds over to the Social Security Administration? They would if they were required by law to do so, and if they were compensated accordingly. The compensation necessary to guarantee each state's adoption of the NST and FICA collections should not be more than the $7 billion we now spend on the IRS for its method of operation (more on this later).

Needless to say, the tax base figure that is arrived at above is an approximation. There are certain amounts of imported business expenditures that will be exempt from taxation, and they have not been factored in. This will *decrease* the base slightly. We can only guess, however, what *increase* in the base will result from our switch from income to consumption based taxing.

What, for instance, will be the effect on the tax base of regaining the $415 billion in capital presently lost every year to compliance costs for the income tax? What effect will result from foreign investment pouring into America? How many hundreds of billions will come to our shores from tax ravaged countries throughout the world as a result of our new tax system and growth-explosive economy? What will be the effect of a rapidly lowering trade deficit? Of plunging interest rates? Of minuscule unemployment figures? Qualls' econometric forecasts are probably well on the conservative side. Real economic growth could easily be much stronger.

A reasoned approach to these facts should tell us that the tax base figure undoubtedly will be *higher* than the above estimate after all decreases and increases are factored in and the dynamics of the new tax system have begun to work their way through the economy. This would allow the rate to be set at 14 or 15 percent. The Schaefer-Tauzin NRST bill (H.R. 3039 presently before Congress) starts with a 15 percent rate which could be achievable depending on how the overall base is determined.

Objection #2 — In order to make a national sales tax work, we would need to tax all services. Experience shows that taxing most services is impractical and will be greatly resisted.

Taxing services has proven to be impractical in other countries and in various states of the U.S. because such taxation is *in addition to* highly punitive income taxes. We must keep in mind that all such punitive taxes will be *abolished* under the NST. The income, corporation, capital gains, estate and gift taxes will no longer be part of our lives. Consequently, taxation on goods and services will not be piled upon existing taxes, but will be *replacing* existing taxes. This will create a much higher public toleration for taxation of "services."

I believe the American people would overwhelmingly welcome a sales tax on all services — utilities, telephone, movie tickets, legal advice, educational help, electrical and plumbing repair, car rentals, funerals, etc. — if it meant *abolishing* the nastiness of the income tax and all the insufferable record keeping and IRS intrusiveness that are part of its implementation.

Since all state sales taxes are *in addition to* federal income taxes, many of their problems will not present themselves under an NST. No country in the past 150 years has promoted the use of a consumption tax as a *replacement* for the income tax. So it is not appropriate to judge the practicality of the NST by recent consumption tax efforts. This is an immensely important point that both Bartlett and Norquist ignore in their condemnation of the NST.

There is a recent precedent in history, however. In 1815 after the Napoleonic Wars, Great Britain had an escalating national debt and a declining standard of living. Wise heads prevailed, thankfully, and convinced Parliament to eliminate the income tax, which ushered in about a fifty year period of growth and prosperity — a period which came to an end when the reinstated income tax of the 1840's became punitive by the 1870's.

Objection #3 — There is a serious problem with intermediate goods and services, which are those resources used in pro duction. They must be exempted, or you get a cascading effect of taxes piled upon taxes.

The method that states use to avoid "cascading" (i.e., issuing resale numbers to businesses so they can exempt all their purchases intended for resale) does create a problem of evasion. For example, a business owner buys an auto for personal use and gives his resale number claiming he is going to resell it. He thus avoids the sales tax. There will be a certain amount of this, but it will not be an insurmountable problem. State sales tax systems are presently functioning with such a method (and state sales taxes are *in addition to* income taxes), so there is no reason to believe a national sales tax that *replaces* the income tax could not function smoothly and profitably.

In his article for *American Enterprise*, Mr. Bartlett writes that to avoid cascading, it would require "tax registration numbers" for businesses exempting them from sales taxes on their business-related purchases. "This immediately creates complications for retailers, as well as easy opportunities for tax evasion.... To fight such cheating, there will have to be a vast auditing procedure that could make today's IRS methods seem tame by comparison." [36]

This is grossly in error. State sales tax systems have used "resale numbers" (or tax registration numbers) for years without complications. It's all part of normally doing business; one's resale number is as innocuous as one's checking account number. Complications are next to non-existent.

Moreover, the state sales tax systems do not require "vast auditing procedures that... make today's IRS methods seem tame by comparison" in order to control the wrongful use of resale numbers. This is because the problem is not of gargantuan dimensions. Mr. Bartlett is reaching strenuously here with his hyperbolic portrayal.

The evasion problem on intermediate goods is managed adequately at the state level because there aren't that many goods that lend themselves to perjuring oneself as to one's intentions (e.g., autos, hardware, office supplies, etc.), and there are not many business owners who seriously attempt to do it. It's one thing to occasionally use a resale number to squeeze some paltry personal hardware items in under tax exempt status, but very few will perjure themselves to evade the tax on major purchases like $20,000 automobiles.

Whatever evasion does occur will naturally lower the tax base. But as we saw previously, a 16 percent NST will bring in a $41 billion surplus over the necessary $639 billion, which means the $4,251 billion base can lose as much as *$256 billion* to evasion and still bring in the necessary $639 billion at 16 percent. An evasion factor in excess of $256 billion is not likely for several reasons. Only the "goods" half of the base is affected here, since "services" are not resold. Moreover, only 20 percent of the population are business owners involved with resale numbers. Even if 30 percent of them use their numbers to seriously cheat (not likely), that's still only 6 percent of the population potentially cheating on one-half of their purchases. In other words, only 3 percent of total consumption would be in jeopardy. Three percent of the $4,251 billion consumption base would be only *$128 billion*. Yet as much as *$256 billion* can be lost to evasion and still bring in the necessary revenue at 16 percent. Bartlett's projection of a 32 to 40 percent rate being needed is totally in error. A 16 percent rate will cover potential evasion.

As far as other forms of evasion are concerned, these also will be "non-problems" under a sales tax. In fact, evasion will be reduced to the barest of minimums across the board.

As Dan Pilla points out in *How To Fire The IRS*, the evasion of income taxes requires a *solitary* illegal act — that of either filing a false return or failing to file a return once a year. In comparison, effective evasion of a sales tax requires the evader to partake in *many* repeated illegal acts (hundreds of them) throughout the year whenever he purchases a good or service. And in addition, he must get the willing compliance of many different merchants with whom he is engaged in trade. The magnitude and difficulty of this will prohibit the evasion of the sales tax on a widespread scale.

Another factor that will greatly inhibit evasion is that there will be no income tax to act as a *motivating reason* for merchant complicity. "At present," Pilla explains, "some citizens are able to induce merchants to make a cash sale, thus avoiding the sales tax. This is possible only because the merchant has something to gain in the process as well. What he gains is the fact that the cash he receives does not show up on his books. Consequently, he avoids the income tax on his profit.

"However, with the elimination of the income tax, the merchant has nothing to gain from assisting in the act of evading the sales tax. In fact, he has everything to lose. State enforcement procedures allow an assessment of uncollected sales taxes to be made against the merchant who failed to collect it." [37]

Thus, it is safe to say there will be less evasion under an NST than we presently endure under the income tax. Evasion will, of course, never be eradicated, but it can be reduced considerably over what we have now.

Objection #4 — Taxpayers will have to keep records and file returns on state income taxes in those states that have them. Thus we will still have to suffer all the invasions of privacy that we now do under the federal income tax.

One major reform at a time. Once we have abolished the federal income tax and its close cousins (corporate, capital gains, estate and gift) then there is nothing to keep those citizens of each state from abolishing their state income taxes also.

In Texas we have no income tax, and we do not intend to enact one. I dare say there would be many states that would emulate our example and repeal their income taxes.

Thus, the American people would indeed be free of keeping records and filing returns. If a certain state wished to retain its income tax, then it should be required to enforce its collection on its own without IRS support. This would greatly diminish the intrusiveness and arrogance of the state collection agents, because citizens can always vote with their feet in retaliation to state government aggrandizement — a luxury they don't possess when subjected to federal arrogance and abuse.

It is the Federal Government's omnipresence and its gestapo-like use of IRS agents that is such a terrible threat to late 20th century America, not the decentralized state governments. To compare state government taxes to the horrid federal income tax, and claim that getting rid of the latter does not solve our problem because we will still, in many cases, have the former to put up with, is indeed a weak and specious reed.

We have a giant, octopus-like monster rampaging throughout our house, sucking up the bounty and meaning of our lives. Because we will still have a few petty rodents left in the house once we have exterminated the monster is hardly reason to abandon our fight against such a creature. The fact that the monster has pledged to hold one of its tentacles in abeyance and "flatten out" its oppression is just one more variant of a long stream of statist ruses that history's oppressors have used to pacify the serfs and keep them docile. Those who fall for such deception deserve, as Benjamin Franklin said, neither liberty nor security.

Objection #5 — Businesses will still have to be audited to ensure compliance with the sales tax due on their production.

They already endure compliance procedures at the state level, so this burden will not be something additional. The legislation enacting the NST will mandate that *state governments alone* act as collectors and that the U.S. Treasury direct its enforcement procedures only at the state governments, not at any individual or business. This means that over 100 million Americans will be totally free of the threat of IRS audits, fines, penalties and record keeping. The fact that the 20 million business owners of America will have to calculate an NST on top of their state sales taxes, and continue to be subject to *state* auditing procedures that they presently are subject to, are very small prices to pay for such freedom.

Moreover, I can't imagine any business owner unhappy with such an additional responsibility. The burden he adds is calculation of a 16 percent sales tax to his accounting procedures; the burden he eliminates is the exploitative harassment that the IRS monolith subjects him to in all his dealings every day of his business life.

Seeing that business owners already calculate such state sales taxes in 45 states, their accounting systems are already in place to accommodate an NST. It's only one more calculation (16 percent of gross sales), and it merely needs to be added to their present procedure. To compare this simple extra calculation to the insufferable, convoluted record keeping and accounting practices that businesses now must endure in order to keep up with the IRS Code is ludicrous. It's like trying to equate one of Aesop's fables to a nuclear physics dissertation. They're both in English, but one is immediately understandable while the other is impenetrable to almost everybody.

Objection #6 — Requiring the states to collect the sales tax assumes that the states will not cheat. It will require compensation (about a 1 percent higher rate) because they don't all have the same base. And because of the cost of facilitating the NST, all states would abandon their own sales taxes and increase their income tax rates to compensate. States without income taxes would immediately adopt them.

States might try to cheat, but hundreds of thousands of individuals try to cheat the system now. So this is not a new problem that we would be creating. In fact, as Pilla shows in his book, we would greatly lessen the containment cost of cheating by reducing the number of payment points from 204 million sources to 50 state governments. What will cost more in money and expertise to enforce — 50 state collection depots that calculate a flat 16 percent rate on gross retail sales, or 204 million individuals and business sources that calculate variable rates on net incomes that can be figured in myriad ways depending on what deductions and exemptions have been granted to or withdrawn from that source's special interest group? Cheating and its containment will be far less of a problem under an NST.

As for compensation to the state governments in return for their collection of the sales tax, Mr. Bartlett's estimate of a 1 percent higher rate is far too high. The national sales tax base will be approximately $4,250 billion. One percent would be *$42.5 billion.* The IRS presently spends *$7 billion* to collect its revenues, and it does its job, like all federal bureaucracies, very inefficiently. The state governments could probably do it for less than $7 billion, even though they would have to hire additional capacity to handle FICA taxes. This is because their auditing and collection procedures for their own sales taxes are already in place. A $7 billion tab would mean one-sixth of 1 percent added to the rate. It would also produce an average of $140 million for each state. I can't image very many states rejecting the necessary collection responsibility if they are to receive $140 million in added revenues for it.

The objection that all states would *abandon* their own sales taxes is not logical. Instead each state would *redesign* their bases to coincide with the NST parameters, thus simplifying their collection procedures.

Income taxes in the states would, on the contrary, not be increased. In many cases they would be abolished. And rather than adopting them, those state governments without them would come under intense pressure to stay away from them. The populace's trust of government is at an all time low for this century, and this is unlikely to change in the foreseeable future. Any state government that tried to increase its income taxes would suffer the problem that California has incurred of late—exodus of its productive people and businesses. Great Britain's "brain drain" of the sixties has come to California of the nineties. And it will come to any other state that is foolish enough to ratchet up its income tax structure.

History very nicely verifies this. As pointed out by Frank Chodorov in *The Income Tax: Root of All Evil,* prior to the Sixteenth Amendment in 1913, it was common for those states without income or inheritance taxes to advertise the fact to the

American people as an enticement for industry to come and settle in their territory. As a result, men and companies of wealth frequently migrated to those states without income or inheritance taxes. This practice acted as a powerful check on the enactment of income taxes by state governments, for no state wanted to lose productive men and companies to resettlement. Because of this, few states adopted income taxes and those that did maintained their rates at minuscule levels. [38]

By eliminating the income tax in favor of the NST, we would restore this very healthy competition among states to attract industry. This would produce precisely the opposite of Bartlett's claim. Individual states would come under pressure to *repeal or greatly lessen* income taxes rather than to adopt them and increase their rates.

Objection #7—Since Congress will most surely exempt certain items so as to help the poor, complexity and potential for evasion is greatly increased. If rebates are used instead to help the poor, you end up with a major entitlement program which will require a significantly higher rate.

Congress will undoubtedly exempt certain items in order to make the NST salable, but the state governments do this also, and it has not caused insurmountable problems. Forty-five state governments have workable sales taxes *in addition to* the federal income tax structure. Therefore, we, as a nation, should certainly be able to implement an NST as *a replacement for* the federal income tax with no insurmountable problems.

As for rebates, the way to handle their inevitable problems is simply to never enact them. Exemption of certain goods and services, yes. Rebates to the general populace, no.

I realize that most plans presently being proposed in the sales tax movement make use of rebates. As explained in the previous chapter, however, I believe such a policy is dangerous and impractical, and it is not necessary. By exempting both food and housing, the burden of the sales tax on the lower income classes is sufficiently lessened. This is all that is needed to make the NST fair. Rebates can only complicate things and grant additional powers to government (e.g., determination and disbursement of hundreds of billions of dollars) that we don't need to be granting.

THE NORQUIST OBJECTIONS

Objection #1 — Any sales tax of 20 to 30 percent will become a VAT within a short period.

The present NST being proposed is a 16 percent rate, which is well under the level that flat tax advocates say is so problematical. In addition, it is a rate that can be moved down toward the 10 percent range over the ensuing years because of the larger tax base resulting from the increased productivity of an economy free of the IRS and disincentives on savings. So the fear that an NST will automatically evolve into a VAT is unfounded.

Those who say a 10 percent rate is unrealistic are probably the same people who thought a Republican takeover of Congress unrealistic. They, no doubt, thought the fall of Communism impossible. Revolution is sweeping the world. A national sales tax would light up the sky of this country production wise. Combine such an explosion of growth with hopefully powerful new voter preferences for extensive reductions of federal expenditures in the next ten years, and a 10 percent NST rate suddenly seems not so "unrealistic."

Once again, we see an ignoring here of the most important aspect of the NST concept: It will be *a replacement for* punitive income taxes. This is 180 degrees opposite to all European sales taxes, which are *in addition to* punitive income taxes. That European sales taxes have evolved into VATs is directly related to this fact.

There is a world of difference in acceptability levels among the people for these two totally different tax proposals. To use the European experience as an example of what we should expect in America is irrational. It would be like saying that since capitalism is having trouble getting launched in Russia, we should not attempt to privatize America's state dominated economic institutions. Russia's underlying culture is so collectivist oriented, and its capital base so impoverished, that it will need many decades to reach a stage of development conducive to a truly free market. Yet America could privatize overnight. And likewise, she could adopt an NST that *replaces* the income tax, while European nations will never be able to implement a sales tax *in addition to* their income taxes.

Objection #2 — A national sales tax would not free us from the burden of paperwork and record keeping. All small business owners would be required to become tax collectors for the state.

Once again, I believe that the small business owners of America would overwhelmingly choose to "collect" the national sales tax rather than "pay" the reprehensible and Byzantine income tax. *Parade* magazine's survey of its readers came back with 96 percent in favor of an NST, 3 percent opposed, and 1 percent undecided. No doubt, a good many of those readers were small business owners.

The flat tax might simplify things, but it will not relieve small business owners of record keeping, deductions, calculations, audits and penalties presently endured. Whatever bookkeeping the 16 percent NST requires, it will certainly be less burdensome than what the flat tax will require, and it will be *sans* the IRS.

Take a poll of any sizeable segment of small business men and women in America. Their answer will be that whatever expense in time and expertise is needed to implement an NST is more than tolerable if it rids the business community of IRS agents and their insane bureaucratic regimentation, their arbitrary penalties and interpretations, their gestapo-like harassment and arrogance, and the perpetual, omnipresent complexity that they create in our business endeavors and record keeping.

Objection #3 — The national sales tax fails the test of making the total tax burden clear. The taxpayer is not aware of precisely how much he pays annually, where with an income tax he knows exactly what he pays every year.

I think we Americans will find the *vague* NST far superior to the *precise* income tax. Our lives will be inestimably saner, happier and more productive with the NST, despite our not knowing "precisely" how much tax we are paying during any given year. We will be reminded every time we purchase a good or service that the 16 percent NST is the price we pay for federal government programs. We will understand that reduction of government spending will be needed to lower that 16 percent rate. This is all the "awareness" we need.

Objection #4 — The national sales tax fails the test of making the tax painful to pay and painful to raise. It would be avoided on large purchases and hidden in the price of small purchases.

What kind of policy is it to seek a tax that is "painful to pay?" Such thinking might be popular with policy wonks inside the Beltway, but it will be hooted out of town in short order by working people throughout the country. Flat taxers may applaud the fact that their tax is more painful to pay, but Americans will choose the *less* painful NST hands down over the *more* painful income tax.

Painful to *raise*, however, is another question. Any tax should certainly be painful to raise, which the NST will be because it will be accompanied by a provision requiring a "two-thirds super majority" of Congress in order for a raise to take place. No serious NST plans are being proposed without such an accompanying provision.

There would be some avoidance on large purchases, but there are massive avoidances now on large income tax bills. No tax system can be designed that will not have an evasion problem. The NST will have a far smaller evasion problem than any other tax, as long as it is limited and subject to being lowered as the base is increased and federal expenditures are reduced. Again, keep in mind, all our experiences of sales taxes being avoided are with sales taxes that are *in addition to* rather than as *a replacement for* punitive income taxes. This one difference will have a significant effect upon people's willingness to pay.

As far as the NST being hidden in small purchases, this is one of those assertions that is not really verifiable and not really very significant. Some people are very aware of the sales tax attached to their purchase; some are not. But who cares? If such obscurity and vagueness are the prices we must pay to rid ourselves of the IRS and the income tax, then so be it. Flat taxers are swatting at gnats and swallowing camels.

Objection #5 — The national sales tax would lead to differential rates and thus special interest groups vying for "breaks" in return for political contributions and campaign support.

The two-thirds vote required in order to raise federal tax rates should protect us against any policy of "differential rates." In order to lessen the rate of one group, Congress would then have to *raise* it for others (or create some other tax) to compensate. Both of these options would require two-thirds of Congress, which will not be easy to achieve.

Keep in mind also, this is not just a problem for a national sales tax; the flat tax has no protection against "differential rates" other than resorting to a two-thirds vote requirement for any tax increase. And differential rates are certainly a potent danger in any form of income taxation. This is what "progressivity" is all about. If flat taxers are worried about Congress' susceptibility to resort to such favoritism in return for campaign support, then they need to look toward buttressing their own models against such a policy, for they are equally if not more threatened by it than the national sales tax.

This, of course, is why a constitutional amendment is necessary for total protection. The accompanying amendment to the NST should mandate a *uniform rate* so there would be no political trade-offs and "breaks" in return for support from special interest groups. All goods and services would have the same rate, and Congress would not be able to tamper with them.

Objection #6 — The national sales tax risks saddling the American taxpayers with what Europeans suffer from, both an income tax and a national sales tax.

If such a danger is a possibility under an NST, then it is also a possibility under a flat tax. Congress could, at any time, pass a sales tax to accompany a flat tax and saddle us with what Europeans suffer from. The flat tax is no less susceptible to such a fate than the NST.

As we saw in Chapter One, we are in danger right now of being saddled with *both* a sales and an income tax. All it would require is a 51 percent vote of our present Congress to enact a small sales tax for assorted "worthy goals," and then gradually increase it over the years. Therefore, replacing our present income tax with the national sales tax does not put us in any danger that we're not already in. In fact, it will reduce the danger of being saddled with *both* a sales and an income tax because it will increase the required vote percentage for raising rates to a two-thirds super majority.

The "two-thirds vote provision" that will accompany enactment of the national sales tax should protect us against the possibility of being stuck with both taxes until a constitutional amendment outlawing all income taxes is enacted. Once the IRS is dismantled and the income tax is reduced to zero, we will certainly be in a stronger position than we are at present.

Congressmen Dan Schaefer (R-Colo.) and Billy Tauzin (R-Lou.), co-chairmen of the National Retail Sales Tax Caucus, point out in a recent press release that just about any objection made against the national sales tax can also be made against the flat tax as well as our present income tax system. This needs to always be kept in mind when one confronts opposition to the NST.

* * *

The reader should now see that the "administrative difficulties" of the NST, claimed by Bruce Bartlett, Grover Norquist and other income tax defenders, are not in the least insurmountable. In fact, in most cases they are not even difficulties. All alleged problems of the NST are either non-problems, or they have solutions far more acceptable to the populace than anything an income tax system can offer.

The NST is an idea whose time has come. As with all policy revolutions, those who have spent years working for or defending an opposing idea (e.g., the flat tax) are going to be upset with the revolution that is being proposed. It is hoped, however, that the great majority of those in the flat tax camp will recognize the superiority of a properly crafted national sales tax and join the battle to genuinely restore America.

The fact that this revolution will not be easily ushered in is no reason to cut and run. A flat tax is nothing but a tiny step in the right direction. The NST is the direction itself. America's destiny is tied up in the vision of our Founders. They strove mightily to give us a government that would *not tax our incomes*. To abandon their vision right when we are so close to victory would be unforgivable.

CHAPTER FOUR

The Real Fight for the Future

The battle lines have been drawn in the tax reform movement. Two distinct philosophies and their advocacy groups are forming: one supporting the status quo of Big Government with its New Deal bureaucracies, and the other vigorously opposing that status quo and working to reduce its power.

The Big Government supporters are an entrenched, elitist array of scholars, politicians, bureaucrats, media pundits, lobbyists, bankers and businessmen — whose lives, in one way or another, are tied to the perpetuation of the mega-state and its Byzantine network of regulations and privileges. They naturally wish to *maintain* the welfare state that has been handed down to us from FDR and LBJ.

In opposition to this elitist array are the free-market advocates — a rapidly growing band of conservative, libertarian and independent Americans who are disgusted with Washington's special interest bureaucracies. They consist of unsubsidized family farmers, non-union blue collar workers, young turk entrepreneurs, old fashioned teachers who believe in basic values, church traditionalists who still hold to the faith, and renegade scholars resurrecting the truths of America's constitutional heritage. They are the new breed free-enterprisers of the 21st century, and are steadfastly determined to restore the principles upon which America was founded. They are fed up, rebellious, and they wish to *dismantle* the welfare state of FDR and LBJ.

Big Government supporters begrudgingly realize the necessity of reforming our tax system. Most of them will admit that it has evolved into a travesty. But their notion of "reform" entails retention of a distinctly *progressive* tax rate that is levied on individual *incomes*. They have no desire to relinquish the policy of "progressivity," because to do so would eliminate the primary impetus for government expansion and the bureaucratization of America's economy. It would destroy the foundation of massive welfarism to which they have tied their ideological allegiances and careers. Thus, they speak the language of political change, but promote the policies of statist accommodation. The tax "reforms" they propose appear on surface to be substantive, but in reality are subtly designed to *maintain* the system and its present political configurations of power in Washington. In their minds, the essence of the centralized welfare state, shored up by a redistributive income tax, is not to be challenged.

Such Big Government supporters espouse either slightly modified versions of our present income tax system with its progressive 15 to 39 percent rate structure (Richard Gephardt's plan), or one of the "flat" tax plans of Dick Armey and Jack Kemp with their progressive 0 to 16 and 0 to 19 percent rate structures.

In contrast to such Big Government supporters, America's conservative and libertarian free-market advocates wish to bring about meaningful tax reform. They understand the need to eliminate "income" taxation, the need to move away from "progressivity," and the paramount necessity of abolishing the "King's revenuers" — the IRS. These dissident Americans realize full well that such a tax reform will radically alter everyone's lives *for the better,* which of course is why they wish to enact the national sales tax instead of one of the flat taxes being proposed. They desire substantive change and a new vision of life for the

21st century. They have no intention of continuing to accommodate the plethora of dinosaur bureaucracies bequeathed to us by FDR and LBJ. They know well that the hemoglobin of the mega-state is the *progressive income tax*, and they intend to strip it of its life blood so that their children and their childrens' children might once again realize the birthright of liberty due all Americans.

The Underlying Motives

It is vital to understand the dynamics lurking behind these two major tax reform movements in America today. Which one of these proposals is accepted (the flat tax or the national sales tax) will determine, to an overwhelming degree, the political and economic nature of our lives in America during the upcoming century. The *flat tax* will lead to a continuance of vast centralized power in Washington because it enhances progressivity and reinforces the IRS. The *national sales tax* will lead to a decentralization of power from Washington out to the local communities and a restoration of freedom to all productive Americans because it reduces progressivity and abolishes the IRS.

The statist establishment (whether it calls itself Democratic or Republican) rightly fears the national sales tax, because such a tax would end the practice of "wealth redistribution" and enable the people of America to *retain their own earnings*. This would put an end to the incessant flow of taxpayer dollars to Washington in order to buy votes from the special interests. This would put an end to the game of "tax and spend" that FDR and LBJ perfected. This would necessitate a wholesale re-evaluation of political goals in America.

The Demopublican establishment in Washington, with its vast array of special interests, does not want to contemplate such a diminution of its power and perks. This is why there has been such a flurry of attacks from both Democrats and Republicans against the national sales tax. Those who have risen to power on the planks of the Great Society's regimental programs do not wish to see those planks dismantled.

Of course, not all legislators and pundits are motivated on this issue by their own aggrandizement. Some are simply misinformed in their evaluation of the national sales tax and need enlightenment. For example, I'm sure that Dick Armey and Jack Kemp support the "flat" tax not because of any desire to expand the welfare state of FDR and LBJ, but because they don't truly understand the revolutionary specifics of the national sales tax, and because they mistakenly believe that the only way to get our tax system changed is to pay obeisance to the liberal establishment's concept of progressivity. Thus, they have been seduced by the notion that large personal deductions ($11,350 and $5,300) are needed in order to be "fair" and get the American people's approval.

I believe both Mr. Armey and Mr. Kemp have bought into a false concept of "fairness." As a result, they have crafted tax plans that are simpler and more conducive to economic growth than the present monstrosity we are burdened with. But such plans will perpetuate the IRS, convey favors to the rich, and create a vast constituency of Americans that pays *zero taxes* for the support of federal government services. This can only further entrench the forces of statism in Washington.

Because of its capacity to raise the deduction levels, Congress will have the power to continually add additional Americans into the *zero tax* category. It needs only to steadily raise the deductions as the base increases over the years. With such a power, how long will it be before Congress has solidified over 50 percent of Americans into a grand FDR-style coalition that supports an ever expanding, centralized mega-state in Washington because it costs them nothing or next to nothing in taxes? Of course, it will be a conservative, fiscally responsible mega-state with a balanced budget. But it will still be a *mega-state*. It will still be intrusive, despotic and unconstitutional.

If our goal is to reduce government, increase freedom and restore equality under the law, then we need to do far more than substitute a conservative welfare state for a liberal welfare state. The spirit of freedom and self-reliance needs to be regained by Americans. The great principles of the Founders, inscribed so eloquently in the Declaration of Independence, must once again be enshrined in the hearts and souls of every citizen. This will require a *dismantling* of the welfare state bureaucracies that dominate our lives, not their *accommodation*.

The present Republican revolution is selling the American people short and cheapening the magnificent purpose of our nation, if it settles for the bland and superficial "Contract With America" — which is nothing more than substituting a responsible mega-state for a wastrel mega-state. The overwhelming need in America today is for men and women to regain their sense of independence and strength of will — that "can do" spirit of entrepreneurship that rocketed us to world leadership in less than a century.

The American dream has never been about security and entitlements. It has always been about *freedom* — the freedom to be our own person, to build our own lives in our own communities, to take care of our own problems in a voluntary marketplace of men and ideas. If Republicans cannot see this indisputable sociological and philosophical fact of life, then they don't deserve to lead America into the 21st century.

Sadly there appear to be many Republicans who cannot see this. These are the Demopublicans — the ones who are now vehemently fighting to save needless welfare state bureaucracies and ensure continued subsidies and favors to the special interests. These are the short-range mentalities who see only that their personal power and status are endangered, which they are now scurrying to shore up even though the country will be denied a desperately needed increase in *freedom* and *productivity* in the process.

Like all entrenched establishments of history who have built their careers upon government usurpation, these Demopublicans will not voluntarily give up their power. They must be stripped of that power by mandate of the people, and the stripping process is going to entail a long, contentious fight. Enemies will be made. Flourishing careers will evaporate. Lives will be altered dramatically. But if America is to restore the meaning of her origin as a nation, then she must not settle for merely a *conservative* mega-state. She must not settle for merely "tinkering around the edges" of the income tax system.

What kind of taxes a country tolerates determines whether that country remains free or succumbs to government regimentation, whether it produces economic abundance or stagnation, and whether its people remain self-reliant or become subservient. All productive citizens of this land must come to realize that if America is to be saved, we as a people must challenge not just the mega-state in Washington that is corrupting our way of life, but the life blood that feeds that monster — the *progressive income tax.*

The Choice Before Us

In 1773, a small band of intrepid patriots, called the Sons of Liberty and organized by Samuel Adams and John Hancock, rowed out into the Boston harbor where they boarded a group of British merchant ships and proceeded to throw overboard thousands of pounds of East India tea in protest to the egregious taxes being levied on them by a far away, tyrannical government.

The Sons of Liberty were supported throughout the colonies by eager sympathizers, yet these bold men and their followers comprised but a small minority of those who inhabited America at the time. Most Americans of the day preferred not to protest British arrogance. They stayed behind closed doors in response to the looming revolution, replying that "it was one's duty to pay his taxes," that "making a fuss over such matters would never get anyone anywhere," that Americans "could learn to adjust to such levies." Rather than join with the rebels, they stayed behind where it was safe and popular, lending their support to the royalist establishment of their day.

This tendency to avoid confrontation has always been the nature of humans throughout history. Whenever tyranny descends upon men's lives, there are those who invariably find excuses to justify its "necessity" and even profit from it, while the intrepid automatically stand against such tyranny, expressing their outrage openly and adamantly.

It takes indelible spirit to challenge an overbearing government that is usurping men's rights. Most men prefer compromise and the warm comfort of social approval, and thus willingly accept the erosion of their freedom while conjuring sophistic arguments to justify their default.

Contemporary America is now confronted with a choice, equatable to that of those who stood with the rebels of Boston in 1773 and those who hid behind closed doors in support of the royalist establishment. Americans will have to choose with which side they wish to stand in today's confrontation.

The term "confrontation" here does not mean fighting in the armed or physical sense, but rather in an *ideological* manner. As long as one's government maintains the democratic process, then armed confrontation can be no sane man's option. We still have the power in this country to galvanize the *minds* of our fellow Americans — to rise up and reform our government through peaceful, educational and democratic means. We are still free to speak, to write and to vote.

We need to remember Thomas Paine's dramatic words: "An army of principles will penetrate where an army of soldiers cannot... it will march on the horizon of the world, and it will conquer."

The battle lines are thus drawn between today's Sons of Liberty and the royalist establishment of Washington. There is no middle ground to seek out, no safe haven of neutrality. The new Sons of Liberty stand for individual freedom and equal rights for all Americans, and thus a *consumption based* tax that is as close to uniformity as possible. The Big Government royalists stand for continued state control over the economy and the dispensing of special privileges to select groups, and thus an *income based* tax that is distinctly progressive.

One of these two tax systems with its accompanying ideology will prevail, and with its prevalence will lie the future of freedom for America. History will judge each of us by which side we choose. The very essence and meaning of our lives are tied up in our choice.

For all men and women who believe in the concepts of limited government and personal independence, the choice is clear: We must pass an amendment to the Constitution that abolishes all forms of *income* taxation, we must establish a limited national sales tax as a replacement, and we must purge forever from our land every last office of the IRS. Until these three reforms are achieved, there can be no hope to genuinely bring the federal Leviathan under control and restore to the American people their lost rights.

Each and every American who loves his country and the free life for which she was formed, must stand and be counted. Our goal is to regain that free life, and we cannot rest until it is attained.

As one of the great economists of the 20th century, Ludwig von Mises, so forcefully reminded us many decades ago: "Everyone carries a part of society on his shoulders; no one is relieved of his share of responsibility by others. And no one can find a safe way out for himself if society is sweeping toward destruction. Therefore, everyone, in his own interests, must thrust himself vigorously into the intellectual battle. None can stand aside with unconcern; the interest of everyone hangs on the result. Whether he chooses or not, every man is drawn into the great historical struggle, the decisive battle into which our epoch has plunged us." [39]

Whether you, the reader, choose to be or not, you are a part of this battle. Even if you choose not to get involved, that in itself is a choice, and it will reinforce the cause of government aggrandizement. Like the royalist defenders in the 1770's who remained behind closed doors, by your silence and default you will have given aid to today's royalist elites who control the political levers of our society — a control in direct contradiction to the constitutional design of the Founders.

"All that is necessary for the forces of evil to win the world is for enough good men to do nothing," declared Edmund Burke during a time of equal crisis in the 18th century. We are no different today. If the good men of America choose to do nothing in face of the Federal Government's usurpation of their rights, then evil will indeed win.

The measure of our strength and our humanity can be gauged by the stands we take during our brief tenure on this earth. There are few issues for which we as Americans will be called upon to fight that will match this one in importance. Historical crises are rarely defined so saliently and decisively around a singular issue. But that is the power of taxation in men's lives. That is the power of this watershed era of American history of which we are a part. We have the opportunity to spectacularly reform our nation for the better. We dare not "stand aside with unconcern." Everyone of us must get involved — for our country, for our children, for truth, for freedom, for equal rights.

Notes

1. Bernard Iddings Bell, *Commonweal*, September 21, 1951, quoted in George H. Nash, *The Conservative Intellectual Movement In America, Since 1945* (New York: Basic Books, 1976), p. 208. Emphasis added.
2. I am indebted here to G. Edward Griffin for his explanation of apportionment and its limiting effect on Congress in "Repeal the Income Tax," *The New American,* February 29, 1988; and also to Bettina Bien Greaves of The Foundation For Economic Education for her historical study, "The Battle of the Income Tax" (unpublished manuscript, 1954).
3. Interview with Congressman Bill Archer, "GOP: Clinton faced change and 'blinked,'" *USA Today,* February 7, 1995, p. 9A.
4. Richard Lugar, Speech in Indianapolis announcing his candidacy for President, April 20, 1995.
5. Jack Anderson, Speech delivered on Capitol Hill to Cato Institute, April 14, 1995.
6. Frank Champagne, *Cancel April 15th!* (Mount Vernon, Washington: Veda Vangarde, 1994), pp. 16 & 20.
7. Paul Craig Roberts, "It's Time To Repeal The Income Tax," *Washington Times National Weekly,* April 10, 1995, p. 32.
8. Quoted in *Help Congress Abolish The IRS* (Dallas, Texas: Government By The People, 1995), Appendix C.
9. Congressman Dan Schaefer, *Rocky Mountain News,* Op. Ed., April 28, 1993.
10. Quoted in *Rising Tide,* September/October 1995, pp. 26-27.

11. The National Commission On Economic Growth & Tax Reform, *Unleashing America's Potential* (New York: St. Martin's Griffin, 1996), p. 110.

12. J. R. McCulloch, *Taxation and the Funding System* (London, 1845), pp. 141-143. Quoted in Charles Adams, *For Good And Evil: The Impact of Taxes On the Course of Civilization* (Lanham, Maryland: Madison Books, 1993), p. 365. Emphasis added.

13. Letter to S. Kercheval, 1816. Saul K. Padover, ed., *Thomas Jefferson On Democracy* (New York: New American Library, no date), pp. 34-35. Emphasis added.

14. *The Statistical History of the United States from Colonial Times to the Present* (Stamford, Connecticut: Fairfield Publishers, 1960), pp. 91, 141, 409, 413.

15. Ludwig von Mises, *Planning For Freedom* (South Holland, Illinois: Libertarian Press, 1980), pp. 151-152. Emphasis added.

16. *The American Almanac, Statistical Abstract of the United States 1995-1996* (Austin, Texas: The Reference Press, 1995, p. 860.

17. Milton Friedman, "Hong Kong vs. Buchanan," *Wall Street Journal*, Op. Ed., March 7, 1996.

18. Daniel J. Pilla, *How To Fire The IRS* (St. Paul, Minnesota: Winning Publications, 1993), p. 203.

19. Laurence J. Kotlikoff, *The Economic Impact Of Replacing Federal Income Taxes With A Sales Tax*, Policy Analysis No. 193 (Washington, D.C.: Cato Institute, 1995), p. 3.

20. Stephen Moore, "The Lean Years," *National Review*, July 1, 1996, p. 39.

21. Stephen Moore, "Ax The Tax," *National Review*, April 17, 1995, p. 38.

22. Pilla, *op. cit.*, pp. 203-204.

23. Ibid., p. 204.

24. Ibid., p. 231.

25. Ibid., p. 215.

26. Daniel J. Pilla, *Why You Can't Trust The IRS,* Policy Analysis No. 222 (Washington, D.C.: Cato Institute, 1995), pp. 22-23.

27. James Bovard, *Lost Rights: The Destruction of American Liberty* (New York: St. Martin's Press, 1994), pp. 259-292.

28. *Unleashing America's Potential,* op. cit., p. 20.

29. Stephen Chapman, "How Flat Tax Forces Can Win," *Conservative Chronicle,* January 31, 1996, p. 3.

30. Pete du Pont, "Tax Laws Discourage Americans from Saving," *Human Events,* November 17, 1995, p. 18.

31. Jude Wanniski, "One Breadwinner Should Be Enough," *Wall Street Journal,* Op. Ed., February 26, 1996.

32. James M. Buchanan, "The Flat Tax: 'Nutty' It's Not," *Wall Street Journal,* Op. Ed., February 22, 1996. Emphasis added.

33. Stephen Moore, "Capitalist Fools," *National Review,* May 20, 1996, p. 41.

34. William E. Simon, *A Time For Action* (New York: Berkley Books, 1980), p.91.

35. John H. Qualls, *The Impact Of A National Sales Tax On The United States Economy* (Manassas, Virginia: Citizens for an Alternative Tax System, 1991), p. 13.

36. Bruce Bartlett, "The National Sales Tax Fantasy," *American Enterprise,* July/August 1995, p. 60.

37. Pilla, *How To Fire The IRS,* p. 232.

38. Frank Chodorov, *The Income Tax: Root Of All Evil* (Old Greenwich, Connecticut: Devin-Adair, 1954), p. 90.

39. Ludwig von Mises, *Socialism: An Economic and Sociological Analysis* (London: Jonathan Cape, 1951), p. 515.

Recommended Bibliography

For those who wish to further pursue the subjects of taxation, political freedom and market economics, here are some recommended books with which to start. I have provided the publishers' addresses and phone numbers for the books and reports not available in book stores.

Many of the selections listed here can be purchased from Laissez Faire Books, 938 Howard St., Suite 202, San Francisco, CA 94103, (800) 326-0996, (415) 541-9780; or The Foundation for Economic Education, 30 South Broadway, Irvington-on-Hudson, NY 10533, (914) 591-7230. These two organizations carry hundreds of important books, both contemporary and older, on the philosophy of a free society. Their catalogues are available upon request at no charge.

Charles Adams, *For Good And Evil: The Impact of Taxes on the Course of Civilization*. A fascinating study of the connection between taxation and the events of history. Clearly demonstrates the predominant role that high taxes have played in the collapse of great nations from Biblical days to modern times. (Madison Books, Lanham, MD, 1993; softcover, 517 pages, $17.95.)

James Bovard, *Lost Rights: The Destruction of American Liberty*. A sweeping exposé of the Federal Government's ever-increasing violations of individual rights — from the tragic arrogance of Waco, to the lawless authoritarianism of the IRS, to the environmental bullies of the EPA. Filled with startling, horrific tales of the "new despotism" stealing over America. (St. Martin's Press, New York, 1994; softcover, 392 pages, $14.95.)

David Burnham, *A Law Unto Itself: The IRS and the Abuse of Power*. An exhaustive examination of the IRS that tears away the "benign public servant" image the agency pitches to the media, showing us instead an Orwellian monster that thinks nothing of terrorizing citizens and corrupting the principles of the Constitution. (Random House, New York, 1989. Available through Laissez Faire Books, 800-326-0996, hardcover, 419 pages, $14.95.)

John Chamberlain, "The Progressive Income Tax," pp. 121-134 in *The Spirit of Freedom: Essays in American History*, edited by Burton W. Folsom, Jr. An excellent account of the ethical, economic and logical flaws inherent in the idea of "progressive" taxation, along with other articles on the concept of freedom. (Foundation For Economic Education, 1994; 30 South Broadway, Irvington-on-Hudson, NY 10533, 914-591-7230, softcover, 212 pages, $14.95.)

George Gilder, *Wealth And Poverty*. An eloquent moral defense of capitalism and the entrepreneur's vital role in the saga of Western individualism. Demonstrates the profound importance of economic freedom and low taxes in order for prosperity to come about. (ICS Press, 1993; 1205 O'Neill Hwy., Dunmore, PA 18512, 800-326-0263, softcover, 327 pages, $14.95.)

George Gilder, *Recapturing The Spirit of Enterprise*. Our wealth as a nation does not come from politicians and bureaucratic economists with hubristic plans to "manage the marketplace," but from the spontaneous ideas and courage of free, creative risk takers. With soaring prose, Gilder paints vivid portraits of today's business pioneers, interwoven with revolutionary insights in the field of economics. (ICS Press, 1992; 1205 O'Neill Hwy., Dunmore, PA 18512, 800-326-0263, softcover, 275 pages, $14.95.)

Martin L. Gross, *The Tax Racket: Government Extortion From A To Z.* A comprehensive portrayal of all the excessive taxes that afflict American citizens today — local, state, federal, payroll, property, sin, license, gas and countless others that plague us. Gross calls for a national sales tax and abolishment of the IRS. (Ballentine Books, New York, 1995, softcover, 319 pages, $12.00.)

F. A. Harper, *Why Wages Rise.* A brief, easy-to-read discussion of the reasons why wages automatically rise when an economy is free. Shows why "capital accumulation" is the most important factor in elevating one's earnings. (Foundation For Economic Education, 1957; 30 South Broadway, Irvington-on-Hudson, NY 10533, 914-591-7230; softcover, 104 pages, $8.95.)

Henry Hazlitt, *Economics In One Lesson.* A wonderful, classic introduction to the arcane world of economics. It gives the reader a clear, non-technical explanation of the glaring flaws in the welfare state view — the most important one being the statist refusal to look beyond the immediate "benefits" of government intervention to its long term disastrous consequences. (Crown Books, New York, 1979; softcover, 218 pages, $10.95.)

Laurence J. Kotlikoff, *The Economic Impact of Replacing Federal Income Taxes With A Sales Tax.* A Cato Policy Analysis that makes use of a computer simulated model to examine America's present savings crisis and how it can be solved by substituting a consumption tax for the income tax. (Cato Institute, 1995; 1000 Massachusetts Ave., N.W., Washington, D.C. 20001, 202-842-0200, paper, 20 pages, $4.00.)

Rose Wilder Lane, *The Discovery Of Freedom: Man's Struggle Against Authority.* An impassioned, beautifully written testament as to what "individual liberty" is, how it developed in history, and why it is so important for human life. (Fox & Wilkes Publishers, 1984; 942 Howard St., San Francisco, CA 94103; 800-678-8070, 415-541-9780, softcover, 284 pages, $12.95.)

A. J. Langguth, *Patriots: The Men Who Started The American Revolution.* An exciting history of how Americans won their independence. Delves brilliantly into the pivotal events, the intrigues, and the towering personalities of the men who launched our original revolt against tyrannical government. Shows how the "love of freedom" animated the heroes of this era — a love that we Americans today must recapture. (Simon & Schuster, New York, 1988; softcover, 637 pages, $14.00.)

Richard J. Maybury, *Whatever Happened To Penny Candy?* A breath of fresh economic air that explains in high school level terms the rudiments of money, and how inflation, depressions, boom-bust cycles, etc., are caused by centralized governments. This is a must book for the beginning student to understand the deceptions in today's statist explanations of the economy. (Bluestocking Press, 1989; P.O. Box 1014, Dept. J, Placerville, CA 95667, 916-621-1123, 800-959-8586, softcover, 125 pages, $9.95.)

Richard J. Maybury, *Whatever Happened To Justice?* An easy-to-read, modern-day classic that shows why a free and stable society must be based upon a higher law than the "positive law" of the courts and legislatures. It must be structured upon the natural moral law inherent in the universe and the "common law" precedents that evolve from it. (Bluestocking Press, 1993; Placerville, CA, 800-959-8586, softcover, 254 pages, $14.95.)

Ludwig von Mises, *Planning For Freedom* (4th expanded edition). A series of essays by the world's greatest laissez-faire economist, showing the harmful results of government intervention into the marketplace. Discusses profits and losses, labor unions, capital accumulation, collectivism in colleges, Keynesian fallacies, and many other issues. (Libertarian Press, 1980, P.O. Box 309, Grove City, PA 16127, 814-422-8001, softcover, 280 pages, $9.95.)

Ludwig von Mises, *Human Action.* An all-encompassing treatise on economics for advanced students. Approaches the subject from the view of men as purposeful, creative beings rather than X's and O's on a graph to be manipulated by government officials. Mises presents a rational defense of the market, explaining why it must remain free of government interference in order for civilization to advance. (Contemporary Books, Chicago, 1966. Available through Laissez Faire Books, 800-326-0996, softcover, 885 pages, $21.95.)

Stephen Moore, *Government: America's #1 Growth Industry.* A compelling portrayal (with overwhelming facts, figures and charts) of the slow asphyxiation of the private sector by Big Goliath Government. If you wish to know why the incomes of American workers are stagnating, here is the reason why. (Institute for Policy Innovation, 1995; 250 South Stemmons, Suite 306, Lewisville, Texas 75067, 214-219-0811, softcover, 111 pages, $9.95.)

Charles Murray, *Losing Ground.* An immaculately documented, empirical study showing that the Great Society welfare programs have been an unmitigated disaster, making matters worse for their poor and minority recipients. An across the board reform and phase out is advocated. (Basic Books, New York, 1986, softcover, 323 pages, $16.00.)

Marvin Olasky, *The Tragedy of American Compassion.* A powerful history lesson in what is wrong with our modern welfare philosophy. Because charity has been taken over by dehumanizing, self-serving government bureaucracies, it is out of control and devoid of the spirit of personalization. Restore welfare to the private sector, and it would once again become humane and manageable. (Regnery Publishing, Washington, D.C., 1992; softcover, 290 pages, $14.95.)

James L. Payne, *Costly Returns: The Burdens of the U.S. Tax System.* A revolutionary look at the destructive effect income taxes have on our economy and the horrendous waste involved in our compliance with them. Shows how the "social costs" of the income tax gravely alter human effort and retard our growth as a people and a nation. (ICS Press, 1993; 1205 O'Neill Hwy., Dunmore, PA 18512, 800-326-0263, softcover, 256 pages, $14.95.)

Daniel J. Pilla, *How To Fire The IRS.* Part Three (pp. 195-254) of this book contains an excellent explanation of the validity and efficacy of the national sales tax. Pilla covers the entire gamut of issues and questions, doubts and oppositions, in a ground breaking analysis. Must reading for a thorough understanding of the NST concept. (Winning Publications, 1993; 450 Oak Grove Parkway, Suite 107C, St. Paul, MN 55127, 800-553-6458, 612-483-6894, softcover, $12.95.)

Daniel J. Pilla, *Why You Can't Trust The IRS.* A Cato Policy Analysis that documents the unreliability of IRS administration and enforcement of the nation's tax laws. (Cato Institute, 1995; 1000 Massachusetts Ave., N.W., Washington, D.C. 20001, 202-842-0200, paper, 30 pages, $4.00.)

John H. Qualls, *The Impact Of A National Sales Tax On The United States Economy.* An econometric study that statistically analyzes the beneficial effects that would result from switching to a consumption tax. Technical and data-intensive material. (Citizens for an Alternative Tax System, 1991; 9401 East St., Manassas, VA 22110, 703-368-6113, paper, 19 pages, $5.00.)

George Roche, *America By The Throat: The Stranglehold of Federal Bureaucracy.* A scintillating analysis of the disease of "governmentalism" that pervades our country, showing why bureaucracy comes about, why it invariably leads to stultification and failure, why it continues to grow, and what we must do to check its demeaning regimentation. (Hillsdale College Press, 1985; Hillsdale, MI 49242, 517-437-7341, softcover, 200 pages, $14.95.)

Murray N. Rothbard, *Making Economic Sense.* A compendium of 111 essays from LvMI's monthly journal, *The Free Market,* rigorously refuting the established "wisdom" of Demopublican statism. Clear, concise explanations of how divorced from reality our "experts" in Washington are on economic matters. (Ludwig von Mises Institute, 1995; Auburn University, Auburn, AL 36849, 334-844-2500, softcover, 421 pages, $19.95.

About the Author

Nelson Hultberg is a freelance writer in Dallas, Texas, and a graduate of Beloit College in Wisconsin, where he studied economics and history. He has managed several businesses of his own and has been active in libertarian and conservative circles for the past 20 years. His articles have appeared in *Insight, The Freeman, The AIER Report*, and the *San Antonio Express-News*. He is presently completing a book about libertarian politics and conservative values in the American tradition.